Economic
Development

Economic Development

John Kenneth Galbraith

Sentry Edition

HOUGHTON MIFFLIN COMPANY BOSTON

The Riverside Press Cambridge

Second Printing, Sentry Edition, C

Published by arrangement with Harvard University Press. Economic Development *is a revised and enlarged edition of Professor Galbraith's book* Economic Development in Perspective, *which was first published by Harvard University Press. A clothbound edition of* Economic Development *is published by Harvard University Press.*

For Ruth and Seymour Harris

Contents

Introduction

PERHAPS a word on the history of this volume will be
an exception to the typically dull tale of how a book
got written and, additionally, throw some light on the
dilemmas of an ambassador in matters of public expres-
sion.

When I went to India in the early months of 1961, I
found myself faced with the problem of how to recon-
cile the requirement that an ambassador must make
speeches with the fact that he has little to say. He cannot make many major policy-making addresses in the
manner made famous (and one judged much enjoyed)
by the late Mr. John Foster Dulles. The State Department in Washington, no doubt quite understandably,
takes a dog-in-the-manger attitude toward policy-making; it may not do it itself, but it doesn't want ambassadors doing it instead. One cannot expound existing policy for, to the extent that this has been articulated, it
usually hasn't yet been cleared by higher authority. In
any case, to talk about existing policy, and thus to reduce
it to hard cold type, will ordinarily be interpreted as
making policy. Thus, by way of illustration, it is our
policy to defend India against the Chinese. But to say

this sends shivers down sensitive spines. A commitment!
The scrupulous do not even speak of the Chinese. They
advert to the Chinese Communist or Peking regime as
distinct from the legitimate Republic of China.

There is a doctrine that an envoy should spend a
great deal of time enlarging on American virtue and
good intentions. That too is wrong. Frequently one
can put something—an appropriations subcommittee
vote, a speech by Richard Russell, race trouble—in better perspective. But one needs to do that at the right moment, not when one happens to have a talk scheduled.
The United States is the best studied country in the
world. All intelligent people have firm opinions about
it. A generalized speech on our virtue will move only
those others whose minds are so pliable that they can
be moved by anything and who, accordingly, will be
batted into some other field the next day. Besides,
speeches on virtue, though they lend themselves to the
diplomatic style, are not highly exciting.

Still, there were the speeches to make. I had not been
warned, for everyone assumes that ambassadors will
make speeches without saying anything.

My solution was to prepare and give a series of lectures on economic development. This was a topic of
which I knew something; it was one of much interest to
Indians. It was an especially good subject for university audiences. A.I.D.—the Agency for International
Development—is tolerant and I could afford not to
worry if it weren't. In the end I gave such lectures
(with some repetition) at the Universities of Madras,
Calcutta, Bombay, Rajasthan, Patna, Mysore, Gujarat,

Jammu and Kashmir, and Lucknow, and at the School of Public Administration of the University of Delhi. By outward evidence the experiment was successful. The lectures were, as I had hoped, reprinted by the newspapers. The crowds in attendance were large and attentive; this was so even at the University of Calcutta where, only a few years before, the appearance of an American ambassador would have brought a reaction paralleling in affection the one Mr. Nixon ultimately found so rewarding at San Marcos. The lectures were extensively discussed.

The humor of college professors is almost invariably bad because they do not realize that students, who are both bored and anxious to flatter, will laugh at anything. What goes over in class thus becomes their standard of wit. The more general response to these lectures was subject to a similar discount: Anything was better than what the long-suffering Indians had come to expect on such occasions. One should not assume anything very brilliant. Still I did not resist when the United States Information Agency moved to publish the first of five of the lectures and when Harvard University Press proposed bringing them out in the United States. I somewhat revised them for these purposes—lectures make bad reading, but fortunately I had written them with newspaper readers rather than listeners in mind— and they were published under the title *Economic Development in Perspective*.

In this volume I have added four more chapters, two of which were written for American audiences and published by *The Atlantic Monthly* (October 1962), and have dropped the word "Perspective" from the title since I am not entirely sure why it was there in the first place. Further revisions have been made not only to eliminate duplication, but to insure that ideas accord with my present view of the problem. In these last years I have had a rich and intimate involvement with the problem of economic improvement in an economically deprived country. There would be grounds for suspicion if, on some matters, I had not changed my mind.

Were I writing this book afresh, there are a few things which I might further change less by way of substance than for emphasis. Thus, I would deal at greater length with problems of economic administration. There is no problem for which intimacy breeds such respect. Indeed one of the important objects of all planning should be to reduce the amount of administration involved. Although I have mentioned it here, I would be even more concerned, especially as regards India, with how a larger part of the task of economic management might be shifted to the price system. At the same time, I would also wish to make it clear that nothing in this argument should cause personal comfort to the vestals of the free market. For in making their case a matter of religious dogma and urging the exorcism of all planning, they have discredited the useful relation which the price system can have to planning. Indeed perhaps only the temperance movement has suffered more from its zealots in this century than the market and there are many remarkable points of resemblance.

This book still bears the stamp of its origins.[1] Each of the chapters was prepared for a separate audience; each accordingly has its own beginning, middle, and end. While I generally had in mind some day to present these various parts as a whole, the plot would have been better had this been written as a book from the first chapter to the last. I trust that the reader will understand or, possibly, be grateful for an excuse for reading only one chapter at a time.

J. K. G.

New Delhi, India
July 1963

---

[1] Because of these origins the revenues of this and the earlier edition have been assigned to Harvard for research and educational purposes.

Economic
Development

I. The Purpose
of Economic Development

ONE OF THE generally amiable idiosyncrasies of man is his ability to expend a great deal of effort without much inquiry as to the end result. Most of the descriptions of the moon which one sees make it out to be a rather unattractive piece of property. The absence of atmosphere would seem to be a real handicap. Even the twenty-foot steps which, with the diminished force of gravity, men will take, though initially interesting, may in the end prove inconvenient for getting around in a small house. Yet these and similar reflections show no signs of deterring man from his effort to get there. And I, for one, am glad that they do not. It is an interesting, if by no means inexpensive, adventure and one that is worth pursuing for its own sake. Evelyn Waugh in *Decline and Fall* tells the useful story of a modern churchman who, while reflecting deeply on the sins of the world, was suddenly impaled by the question of why God had made it in the first place. Thenceforth he could think of nothing else. He had to give up his church; the only further employment he could find was as chaplain in a progressive penitentiary where, per-

haps mercifully, he was soon murdered by another
deeply thoughtful man. It is a warning against excessive introspection.

But while appreciating the dangers, it may still be
useful on occasion to ask about goals, and I am
persuaded that this is one such time. For some fifteen
years the world—East and West, capitalist and communist, democratic and more democratic (no country has
lately described itself as undemocratic, much less anti-
democratic)—has been engaged in what it has agreed
to call economic development. And it is now pursuing
this effort in what, with no excess of pessimism, it has
chosen to call the Decade of Development. Development is in active voice; it implies movement toward
some result. We need to reflect on the result. There is
always danger that, in the absence of such specification,
we will risk unintended consequences or act inefficiently
in light of what we really want.

One reason it is necessary to specify the goals of development is that circumstances in the economically
advanced countries have enabled them to remain largely
unaware of the need for choice. The principal purpose
of the economic system, as these countries see it, is to supply a full range of consumers' goods. The particular mix
—the distribution of capital and manpower to different
products—is given by distribution of income and the
efficiency of markets. And if the distribution of resources between, say, necessaries and luxuries—between mass products for the masses and the more pre-
cious and esoteric delights of the few—seems wrong, the

thing to change is the distribution of income. An increase of taxes on the incomes of the well-to-do or the products they consume has anciently been thought the appropriate remedy.

Given the income distribution, the only need is to make production as efficient as possible and insure that markets so function as to reflect faithfully the desires of consumers. All of this being regarded as natural, there has been little tendency, at least in peacetime, to reflect on alternative economic goals. Moreover, there has been a further measure of concurrence from the Soviet-type economies. The Soviet Union has repeatedly proclaimed that its industrial goal is to "catch up" with the United States. By implication, at least, this means a similar industrial apparatus in the service of similar ends. The Soviet goal is, it would appear, to live as much as possible as do middle-class Americans. It has been easy to assume that the industrial apparatus of the United States, Western Europe, and the USSR is the natural and indeed the only model for the newer countries. They need only to re-create in some rough form what the more developed countries already have. Development is the faithful imitation of the developed.

In fact, this is not a proper or useful procedure. There is, first, a very large population very near or sometimes below the margin of subsistence. Those who are hungry have a special claim on resources. So do the measures which promise to remedy privation. There is, for the same reason, a special case against waste or the luxury consumption of the well-to-do. Certain claims of the state take on an added, or seemingly added, urgency in the poor country—a point to which I will return. The question of how much should be consumed now and how much should be invested for larger production and consumption later on assumes a vastly greater urgency, for in the poor country the necessary saving may have to come from people who are already insufficiently supplied. That there must be a conscious decision to conserve resources and apply them to the highest priority needs is reflected in the wide acceptance of the notion that development must be in accordance with a plan.

It is when we come to inspect these plans in their various degrees of sophistication that we find the conflict in goals. To systematize matters, I think we can recognize three types of economic development which are, currently, more or less in vogue. They are as follows:

1. *Symbolic Modernization.* This is designed to give the developing country the aspect, though not necessarily the substance, of development. There are certain things the modern state must have. Any claim to nationhood requires a decently glittering airport, a capital with pavement, some impressive buildings of state, a diplomatic corps, one considerable hydroelectric project, perhaps the intention of creating a steel industry and perhaps also, in practice, a balance of payments deficit. I do not discount the importance of these symbols—or some of them. Certainly no one should be lofty or patronizing about them. Effective national leaders have always known the importance of the concrete and visible expressions of national being. Abraham Lincoln insisted, during the American Civil War, that work on the then

unfinished Capitol continue. It was hardly an essential expenditure, but, as he said, if the legislative building went on, people would feel that the Union would go on. In the last century, American settlers had no sooner redeemed a new county from the wilderness than they went into debt to build an impressive courthouse. Thus, they proved to themselves and to the world that civilization had arrived in this part of Nebraska.

Yet it will be clear that the economic well-being of the people is not much advanced by symbolic modernization. And it may be retarded for those who must pay the bill. In the past, moreover, much symbolic modernization has been a strategy for fooling people into believing something was being done. Or it has been a form of monument building by which politicians have undertaken to commemorate their existence (and perhaps ultimately their inadequacy) at the public expense. As it would be unwise to deny a role for symbolic modernization, so it would be unwise to accord it unqualified approval.

2. *Maximized Economic Growth.* I come now to a more respectable formulation of the goal of development and the one which reflects most strongly the influence of Western economic thought. This proclaims it to be, over some period of time, the greatest possible increase in total and per capita income and product. While, through import restrictions and duties and domestic excises, the production of some less essential goods may be discouraged, the goal is the overall increase in output. The composition of the product is secondary. At the extreme, plan outlays are selected in

accordance with their capital-output ratios. This means that the only test of an investment outlay is the amount by which it increases total product.

There is also likely to be a strong emphasis on heavy initial capital investment. This establishes a large industrial base which then makes possible a larger subsequent rate of expansion in investment goods, consumer goods, or both.

Other questions are decided on similar grounds. The rate of needed savings—voluntary, earned, or imposed through taxation—is set so as to sustain the largest possible rate of growth. And questions of priority that are beyond the statistics available for calculation of capital-output ratios—the position to be accorded education, health improvement, or other social overhead investment —are decided in accordance with their assumed, and sometimes sadly underestimated, contribution to growth, for there is a tendency in our time to think that what cannot be measured isn't much good. The only other test which enters with high respectability is the possibility of economizing in foreign exchange. A slower rate of growth may be acceptable if it permits of increased reliance on internal as distinct from imported resources.

As compared with symbolic modernization, this test of increased income and product obviously has much to commend it. The reality of economic advance—the production of goods and services—replaces the mere image. We have solid and objective tests of performance.

Yet this goal too is not without dangers. People, especially poor people, are not especially influenced by economic gains in the abstract. It is what they can use and enjoy that counts. Considerable extremes of wealth and income continue to exist in nearly all of the less developed lands. These can create a strong drag of demand in the direction of higher-priced or luxury products. And this tendency is especially insidious for many of these products are commonplace in the standard of living of the more advanced countries and equally so, and for that reason, in the consumption habits of the upper-income minority of the poorer country. To the extent that the high incomes of the minority draw development resources into privileged consumption, social differences are widened, and to the strains associated with poverty may be added those associated with obvious differences in well-being. People may come to sense that economic development is not for the many but for the few.

There are further dangers. In the strategy of modern development, taxation—what has come to be called fiscal savings—plays a considerable role. In the less developed land, there is also some likelihood that taxation will fall rather heavily on the poor who, after all, are available in the most abundant supply. And since the underdeveloped country is, *pro tanto,* an agricultural community, there may be a traditional tendency for this taxation to fall upon the farmer or his land. Thus, not only does undifferentiated growth tend to support higher-income consumption, it may do so partly as the result of saving from lower income consumption.

Moreover, the process of development itself both

requires and justifies a substantial increase in the number of people earning higher incomes. Even, perhaps especially, if development is under socialist auspices, there will be a marked proliferation of administrators, managers, engineers, technicians, accountants, clerks, and other civil servants all at rates of pay that seem high to the taxpayer. The political consequences of this may be discomforting in any case. If these jobholders are engaged in forms of development that do not benefit the taxpayer, it will obviously be worse. The latter quickly comes to think of development as something which rewards not him but some urban official.

Finally, there are serious dangers in the heavy investment. The saving that this requires can easily reflect the preferences of the planner, not the people. Since World War II in a number of countries—Hungary, Poland, and most recently it would appear in China—there have been revolts or considerable protests against rates of saving and investment in excess of what the community would endure.

3. *Selective Growth.* The foregoing problems have not gone unrecognized, although the recognition has, perhaps, been less explicit than might be wished. Back of much development planning has been the belief that benefits must accrue as a matter of priority to the more needy sectors of the population. Resources so painfully conscripted from the people must return benefit to the same people.

This politically salutary principle has, however, led to diverse and even contradictory conclusions as to application. To some, agriculture, agricultural extension, community development, and local primary education have seemed the obvious answer. These have acquired a kind of mystique as development for the people at large. But to others the obvious answer has not seemed to be increased agricultural income and amenity. These are only palliatives. Agricultural development, in this view, is primitive, even reactionary. The real answer is industrial employment. This argues for investment in manufacturing, power, transportation, and the other components of an industrial base. The progressive solution is to rescue people, if not from the idiocy, at least from the inevitable poverty of rural life.

This, however, is a policy without appeal to those who remain unrescued. It means, moreover, that there is a period of heavy saving without a reward in consumers' goods even for the urban worker. This has led to political strains paralleling and not wholly distinct from those associated with investment for rapid growth.

In some countries, notably in India, there is further disagreement between those who defend modern machine methods and those who contend that, since employment is the goal, labor-intensive enterprises, including rural and cottage industries of various kinds, should be favored.

This discussion, it must be stressed, is quite apart from the debate over which kinds of investment will lead to the most rapid rate of growth. Thus, although there is wide agreement on a policy of selective economic growth, there is very little agreement on what should be selected.

There is a further development goal which I believe
resolves the foregoing difficulties. It is one that has
been implicit in a good deal of past Indian thinking,
and in the best planning in other countries. This goal
anchors economic development to the consumption requirements, present and prospective, of the typical
citizen—to the consumption, statistically speaking, of the
modal consumer. It organizes development around the
living standard of this consumer and recognizes that his
wishes must be consulted in sacrificing present consumption to future increase. By way of illustration,
if, as in India, the annual income of eighty percent
of all family units is less than R.1200 (about $250),
development resources will be concentrated on consumption that is purchasable by people with such
income. The number of goods and services is not
large. Obviously it means a major emphasis on food,
clothing, shelter, education, and medicines since these
are the dominant items in the economy of the low-
income family. The same rule operates equally against
automobiles, expensive dwellings, luxury consumers'
goods in general. It will be observed that this is not a
decision for agriculture or for industry or even for light
industry as opposed to heavy industry. Industry there
will be, but it is industry which supplies the typical or
modal citizen. That person wants, perhaps first of
all, an abundant supply of inexpensive food. But back
of an improved agriculture lie fertilizer plants and a
chemical industry and well-designed agricultural imple-
ments and an efficient transportation system and hence
a source of steel. Textiles, bicycles, and other low-

budget consumers' goods will similarly command capital investment. More expensive consumers goods will not.

The goal I am here delineating—it might be called the Popular Consumption Criterion—will be seen to resolve the political problems which arise in connection with other criteria. The attention of planners and of planning is kept concentrated on the needs of the most numerous or typical citizen. The chance that he will have any sense of neglect is thus minimized. There is a warning in this system against measures to enhance savings which depress or unduly postpone this citizen's hopes for improved well-being. His own wishes as to his consumption, as opposed to those of his grandchildren, will be respected. We have firm criteria for discouraging luxury imports, production, and consumption. We also have a useful barrier to outlays for symbolic modernization. The taxes for this may reduce popular consumption. Even if they do not, opportunities for investing for such consumption are foregone.

The application of the popular consumption criterion cannot be total. In the past, the poorer countries of the world have often produced the luxury products of the more affluent lands. Exports are still necessary, and while exports can be regarded as a way of getting more urgent goods must economically, export and domestic markets are never wholly separate. What is supplied to one will always, in some measure, be available to the other. And even development that is firmly geared to the income of the modal consumer produces higher incomes. There is no form of development—capitalist, socialist, or communist—which does not accord higher rewards to trained and educated or to otherwise qualified or experienced people. There will, then, be production to meet the purchasing power of these income recipients. This must be recognized and expected.

The criterion is no less important for this reason. For it still fixes objectives and establishes the priorities in the distribution of planned investment. It establishes the line between that which is automatically included and that on which falls a burden of proof. It also provides the basic guide in taxation and in the administration of exchange-controls. Such guidelines, not perfection in their application, are the most urgent need of modern development planning.

II. The Causes of Poverty

As NOTED in the last chapter, among the enterprises currently enlisting the energies of man, one of considerable moment is his effort to launch himself across space. A second, less grand, less costly, but not perhaps less important, is the effort to improve the position of those who will stay behind. My purpose in this and the following chapters is to consider the way in which we are tackling the second of these tasks and the possibility for improvement. That such a possibility exists is evident from a fairly cursory comparison of efforts at the conquest of poverty with efforts at the conquest of space.

Space travel, we take for granted, will be undertaken only after the most comprehensive consideration of the problems to be solved. In the case of a journey to the moon, provision of the energy requisite for escape from the earth; protection from radiation, extremes of temperature, tedium, and other hazards and discomforts en route; the arrangement of an unclimactic arrival; arrangements for a return journey by those unattracted by permanent settlement; and, quite literally, a thousand other things, are all, one is assured, the subject of the most minute calculation. Nor is anything that is vital slighted because of a shortage of money. The knowledge that such care is being exercised will, one imagines, lessen, even if it does not entirely eliminate, the personal misgivings of the first passengers.

Our approach to national poverty, by contrast, is more casual. All prophets of the commonplace aver that something should be done about it. But, remarkably, we have no agreed-upon view or even any strong consensus as to why it exists. Over the last two centuries we have had an active and increasingly sophisticated discussion of the forces which influence economic growth—that is to say, the factors making for increases in total and per capita income and well-being. Without exception, this discussion—of incentives to effort, means for encouraging saving and capital formation, ways of promoting technological advance—applies to societies that are already in process of growth. But the central feature of the poverty-ridden community is the absence of any tendency to improvement. There is stagnation in output and income, and this perpetuates itself year after year and from generation to generation. One cannot extend the analysis of the advancing society to this stagnation. And of the stagnation, we have no analysis.

What we do have is a large—in fact, an astonishing —number of assumptions as to what is wrong. It is upon these assumptions, many of them self-contradictory and all of them of limited applicability, that we have based remedial action. One consequence of our planning is that within the next few years men will reach the moon, and hopefully the righteous among them will return, but the most acute problem of this planet will remain unsolved. If this seems pessimistic, let me list the causes to which, depending on ideology, personal preference, convenience, and even pure accident, we now attribute the poverty of nations and to which we relate our remedies.

1. *The people are poor because they prefer it that way.*

Poverty, in more formidable language, reflects the value system of the people.

This is persuasive. Few Americans have looked at an Asian or African country without reflecting (and commenting) on the favorable effect a little American ambition would have. Nor is the tendency ours alone. Visitors to the central Asian republics of the Soviet Union are told by Russians that the local people are backward because they are lacking in ambition. Yet there is scarcely a country in the world where people do not want economic improvement, where, indeed, it is not a political imperative. We must also remember that Kipling's Englishman dismissed the sorry state of the undeveloped country with an easy wave of his hand and the observation: "The natives are bloody lazy, you know." When it is so couched, we indignantly reject such spurious anthropology.

2. *The country is naturally poor.*

This seems the obvious answer where the soil is sparse and unwatered, the forests thin and the subsoil barren. How could Bedouin or Navaho be rich? But this is an

explanation which badly explains the wealth of Switzerland or the comparative wealth of Israel, both states
that are poor in natural resources. It leads one to won-
der why West Virginians, who live in a state phe-
nomenally rich in natural resources, should have incomes far below those of an arid and barren state such
as Wyoming.

3. *The country is poor because it has been kept in a
state of colonial oppression.*

Over great parts of the world, this is the most
evocative of explanations. The British, French, and
Dutch were in business not for their subject peoples
but for themselves. The people still pay for these centuries of indifference, exploitation, and neglect. Moreover, in an awkward inversion of historical process, some
of the least progressive of the colonial regimes, Portugal
being the notable example, have, on the whole, lasted the
best. The greatest neglect or oppression is being the
longest endured. Yet, again, there are obvious difficulties. In many parts of the world—Latin America
comes immediately to mind—colonialism is far in the
past, but poverty continues. And elsewhere—in Australia, Canada, the United States—colonial rule did not
exclude a considerable measure of contemporary pros-
perity. British India, the part of India where British rule
was the most comprehensive and lasted the longest time,
is today measurably the most progressive part of the subcontinent.

4. *Poverty is the consequence of class exploitation.*
The counterpart of the poverty of the many is the
opulence of the few. The second is the cause of the first.

This explanation is supported by a formidable dialectic and confirmed by arithmetic and observation. Few poor countries are without a minority of exceedingly rich. And it is difficult to understand why an Andean or Middle Eastern peasant should seek to enhance his income by irrigation, improved seed, or acceptable livestock when he knows that anything in excess of subsistence will be appropriated by the landlord, tax collector, moneylender, or merchant. Yet the world has much poverty without evident exploiters. In India and Pakistan there are millions of small land-owning peasants who are very poor but whose poverty cannot readily be related to the enrichment of any landlord, moneylender, tax collector, or other visible oppressor.

5. *Poverty is caused by insufficient capital.*

This seems self-evident. Low income allows of no saving. Without saving, there is nothing to invest. Without investment, there can be no economic advance, and so poverty is self-perpetuating. Yet in Iran, Iraq, and Saudi Arabia, as also in Venezuela, oil provides a rich source of revenue, and capital is not scarce. But the vast majority of the people remain exceedingly poor.

6. *Overpopulation is the cause of poverty.*

In the typical village of India, as elsewhere in Asia, there is rarely enough work to go around. Fewer hands could and would do the same work. If the population were smaller, each person would have a greater share. Yet in other countries everyone works at full capacity for the little he gets. If the worker went, so would his contribution. Since others could produce no more, the share of each would remain much the same. And, as a matter of practical observation, though poverty is often associated with dense population, it is also often associated with sparse population. The Amazon Basin is very sparsely populated and very poor. Southern Brazil is much more densely populated and much more prosperous.

7. *Poverty is caused by incompetent economic policy.*

The poor country, it is argued, is infirm in its commitment to free enterprise. Alternatively, it has not seen the inevitability of socialism. Inflation is the enemy of economic advance. Alternatively, the fault lies with excessively orthodox efforts to stabilize prices and currency.

Practical experience in the less developed lands certainly induces respect for well-considered economic policy. But it is evident that the foregoing explanations of poverty involve an awkward element of internal contradiction. Moreover, the most prominent fact about the very poor country is not that it has free enterprise industry or socialist industry but that it has no industry at all. And inflation which is chronic, especially in Latin America, is invariably a symptom of more deeply seated disorders. Specifically, too much income is being claimed by people who contribute nothing to the total. Until their claims are curbed, inflation is probably less to be feared than stabilization. In any case, there is a mildly ludicrous quality about policy based on this diagnosis. In Latin America in recent times, when inflation is severe, the best and most solemn experts recommend stabilization. When this causes too much pain, a certain easing up is allowed. Under either policy, the poverty remains.

8. *Poverty is caused by ignorance.*

It is a plausible axiom that no literate population in the world is really poor and no illiterate population is otherwise. Yet here one encounters the question of how a poor and illiterate people goes about providing itself with a school system. Whence will come the resources? Poverty may well be a cause of ignorance. But surely it is also a result.

The list of commonly accepted causes of poverty is by no means complete. We regularly attribute some role to the slow rate of transfer of technological knowledge. People cling by preference to primitive and poverty-inducing methods of agriculture and industry because they have not been apprised of anything better or prefer it that way. We also attribute something to war, rapine, predacity, and civil disorder. The Fourth Crusade, Genghis Khan, and the brothers Pizarro showed that, in the hands of highly qualified practitioners, these can have an enduring effect on income. The communities which were the principal objects of their attention have been poor ever since.

One could go on. But the point is sufficiently clear. We have a great many causes of poverty; nearly all are in some measure convincing and all are partially unconvincing. Such is the diagnosis. Yet to prescribe on the basis of any one of these causes must obviously be dangerous. If ignorance is the cause of poverty, to provide capital for power plants or plows will miss the point. If poverty is caused by the oppression of landlords, provision of improved seed will do no good. Why reform one's farming for the benefit of somebody in

Lima, Quito, or Paris? It is pointless to urge a population policy if overpopulation is not the problem, but all
other gains can obviously be annulled if overpopulation is the problem. It does no good to control inflation
if stabilization serves only to reveal the underlying
problems of the society in even harsher form. So long
as we have no diagnosis of the poverty of a country, we
can surely have no cure.

We can say something about the diagnosis, however.
It is useful, first of all, to see national poverty as the
product of a plurality of causes. And several causes will
normally operate in any country. These will vary with
culture and historical antecedents. The causes in Latin
America may be fairly similar. We should expect that
between Latin America, the Asian subcontinent, Africa,
the Middle East, the difference in the admixture of cause
will be very great. And so it is.

If we recognize a diversity of causes, we will take an
eclectic view of remedies. This means that we will not
allow dogma to govern prescription. One of our advantages, potentially at least, over the Soviet design for
economic development is a greater freedom from con-
trolling doctrine. Hence we have or can have a greater
capacity to adjust remedies to cause. We would do well
to protect that advantage.

We can also, with effort, avoid selecting remedies for
their convenience. There are some presumptive
remedies for poverty that come much more readily to
hand than others. Technical assistance in the form of
improved seed or advice on organizing farm cooperatives
is infinitely easier to provide to farmers than land re-

form. A hydroelectric power project is much easier to launch than a sound system of elementary education. To provide an effective system of public administration for people newly emerging from colonial rule—in the Congo, for example—is a peculiarly baffling task. Convenience, in the past, has played a large part in the choice of remedies. Yet if a bad land system, mass illiteracy, a corrupt, incompetent, or exiguous public administration, or all three are what is wrong, the provision of technical aid or the damming of rivers will do little good. If technicians and capital are the real shortages, provision of technicians and capital will do great good.

Such are the gains of examining each case on its merits. Yet some generalization about the problem of national poverty is inescapable. In pleading for clinical examination of each country or area, one could easily urge long study and much delay in a world that is clamoring for action. And there is one generalization that is reasonably safe. People are the common denominator of progress. So, *paucis verbis,* no improvement is possible with unimproved people, and advance is certain when people are liberated and educated. It would be wrong to dismiss the importance of roads, railroads, power plants, mills, and the other familiar furniture of economic development. At some stages of development—the stage that India and Pakistan have now reached, for example—they are central to the strategy of development. But we are coming to realize, I think, that there is a certain sterility in economic monuments that stand alone in a sea of illiteracy. Conquest of illiteracy comes first.

Similarly, our Latin American policy is coming gradually to recognize that economic liberation is the first step to economic advance. Until people have a part in economic progress, there will be no economic progress. It will take time to convince everyone, both at home and abroad, of this often inconvenient fact. Some will continue to urge that no boat be rocked or that we buy our way around reform. Others will continue to hope that privilege, however disastrous, will at least last out their own lifetimes. A certain number of our officials will continue to believe that the well-spoken, respectable, and conservative people whom they see, hear, understand, and entertain are designated for survival by a socially discriminating God. Nevertheless, one senses a growing recognition that social justice is indispensable for social progress.

This is very modest reassurance. The space travelers are well ahead of those who grovel in the problems of this planet when it comes to the techniques of problem-solving. In regarding our diagnosis of the problem of national poverty, we should, paraphrasing Winston Churchill, be modest and realize that we have much to be modest about.

I turn now to prescription.

III. The Choice

THE COUNTRY entering currently on nationhood is faced, at least in principle, with the interesting problem of selecting an economic system. The choice, one from which the developing countries of the eighteenth and nineteenth centuries were conveniently exempt, is between the economic, political, and constitutional arrangements generally associated with the Western democracies, on the one hand, and the policy and economic organization which avows its debt to Marx and the Russian Revolution, on the other.

These are not homogeneous alternatives. Poland, where the agriculture—and hence close to half the economy—remains in private hands and subject to market influences, differs radically in economic structure from the far more completely socialized economy of the Chinese mainland. In Scandinavia, the United Kingdom, and India, the word socialism is politically evocative. As a result, politicians try to find as much of it as possible. In the United States, measures that would elsewhere be identified with socialist enlightenment—social security, agricultural price guarantees, even the public development of public power sites—are defended as making private enterprise function better.

Also, one must be a trifle cautious in speaking of a choice. Geography and the proximity of military power have had much to do with the decision. Had Poland, to select a country not unaccustomed to movement, been more radically relocated after World War II to, say, the position of Paraguay, its political reorientation would have been by, perhaps, 179 degrees. Individuals commit themselves as a matter of free choice to a Marxian political and economic design. But nations have rarely done so in the normal course of unmanaged elections, a reluctance which was foreseen by both Marx and Lenin.

Nevertheless the broad alternatives exist. My purpose now is to weigh their advantages from the standpoint of the developing country. I am aware that an American ambassador will not be considered by everyone a wholly impartial judge. There would doubtless be eyebrow-lifting by captious people if my evidence were to lead me to the wrong conclusion.

But the choice merits serious assessment. The bulk of the present literature on economic development consists of proclamations of superiority by one side or the other. We share with the Communists a faith in the persuasive value of robust unsupported assertion. Were the advantage all on our side, we would have no reason to worry. But we do worry. So a moderately unemotional appraisal of what we have to offer the developing country as compared with the Communists might be useful.

The goal of the developing country, we remind ourselves, is to bring itself as rapidly as possible into the twentieth century, and with the apparatus of individual and group well-being—food, clothing, education, health services, housing, entertainment, and automobiles—which is associated in every mind, urban and rural, bourgeois and Bolshevist, with twentieth-century existence. A few, but only a few, demur or attempt, as in the first chapter above, to give the goal more specification. Not even the most monastic Christian, the most contemplative Buddhist, or the most devout Gandhian can be considered completely secure against the charms of the bicycle, motor scooter, or transistor radio.

Differences between the two broad designs for development are not difficult to detect. The problem is to identify those that are decisive, that make the difference between change and stagnation, success and failure. Of these critical differences there are three. The first is in the diagnosis of the causes of poverty and the related remedy. The second is in the way development is organized. The third is in the political and constitutional environment of development. I now take up these differences.

Each of the systems drastically simplifies the causes of poverty and then proceeds to act on the basis of this simplification. In the Marxian view, poverty is caused principally by institutions which chain the country to its past—which hold it in colonial subjection, allow the exploitation and subjugation of the masses, deny the people the reward of their labor, make government not the efficient servant of the many but the corrupt handmaiden of the few, and which, in the aggregate, make any important progress impossible.

The Western view, as I have noted in the last chapter, is amorphous. But in what may be called the working view, the poor are considered the victims of their poverty. All societies have capacity for growth, but the poor society has nothing with which to buy growth. Having less than enough for its current needs for food, clothing, and shelter, it has nothing for investment in education, improved agriculture, transportation, public utilities, or industrial enterprise.

Each of these views leads naturally to a prescription. If institutions hold a country to its past, the answer is the destruction of those institutions. If the problem is the self-perpetuating character of privation, the answer is to provide the catalyzing resources—specifically, economic aid and assistance in its use—which the country cannot supply to itself.

Here is the first difference: The Marxian emphasis is on institutions which inhibit progress and the need to eliminate them; our emphasis is on the self-perpetuating character of poverty and the catalyzing role of aid. Each system, we should note, has a cause and an accompanying remedy that are not without convenience to itself. The Soviets have always been short of capital, but they have had a revolution which could be exported at moderate expense. Accordingly, they found it convenient to associate backwardness with colonialism, feudalism, and repressive capitalism, all of which could be eliminated by revolution. By contrast, capital for us has been comparatively abundant. We could export it with comparative ease. On the other hand, American advocates of social revolution—of land reform, the elimination of feudal privilege—especially if in public office, often risk a measure of political reproach.

The second difference between the systems is in the way development is organized. Although there is room for some national preference, and heresy cannot be entirely eliminated, the Marxian commitment is to state ownership of the means of production—of land, capital plant, and natural resources. Private ownership of productive resources and their use for private gain is, in fact, considered one of the retarding institutions. The elimination of private ownership normally leaves the state in possession. Pecuniary incentives to individual and group effort are much used. But incentives which employ the device of property ownership to combine reward for individual effort with reward for the efficient management of property are excluded in principle, and, in large measure, in practice.

The non-Marxian design for organizing development is not so easily typed. In the past, many countries—Japan, Germany, Canada, and, to a remarkable degree also, the United States—have made state ownership of canals, turnpikes, railroads, electric power and other utilities, and even steel mills the fulcrum of development policy. India, Egypt, and some South American countries are doing the same today (and are being lectured on occasion by those Americans who are unaware of their own history, on the ideological unwisdom of their course). However, the main, and indeed over-

whelming, reliance in non-Marxian development, both
in agriculture and industry, has been on private ownership of productive plant. This is even true of countries
such as India which nevertheless prefer to describe themselves as socialist.

The choice is thus between a comparatively firm commitment to public ownership of productive plant and
resources and a blurred commitment to some combination of public and private ownership in which practical
considerations as well as ideology determine the precise result. This is not a sharp distinction, but clearly it
is one which has meaning. Let me now turn to the
practical consequences of the foregoing distinctions.
There is, we may note, a good deal of experience on
which to draw.

Two major advantages lie with the Western or non-
Marxian alternative. There is, according to ancient
physical law, a certain difficulty in extracting blood
from a stone. This is, in all respects, comparable with
the problem of getting savings out of a poor society.
When people do not have enough to eat, they are loath
to forego any part of their meal that they may eat better in the future. Pleas on behalf of a better life for
children and grandchildren leave the man of simple,
uncomplicated intelligence unmoved; he reflects that
starvation will prevent him from having any viable
children and, *pro tanto,* grandchildren either. But
Marxian no less than non-Marxian societies must have
savings; without them there can be no growth. Accordingly, the Western pattern of development, with its

prospect of assistance from outside the country, eases one of the most painful problems of development. This is why economic aid has become such an important feature of Western foreign policy. It is the process by which savings are transferred from countries where saving is comparatively unpainful to those where it is very painful. It exploits one of the major advantages of our system.

To be sure, the Communist countries are not without resources in this respect. The Soviet Union, though its capacity has been far less than ours, has spared some savings for other countries. Communist economic and political organization deals more effectively—or ruthlessly—with unproductive and excessively luxurious consumption. Such consumption by a small minority is, as I have noted, a common feature of the poor country. And Communist organization can, within limits, squeeze blood from its turnip.

The penalty is the pain, and this cannot be avoided. The rioting in Poland in 1956 which brought Gomulka to power was occasioned in large measure by the enforcement of a rate of saving that was too stern for the people to bear. These last years on the Chinese mainland have evidently been years of serious trouble and tension. Part of the problem is related to the socialist organization of agriculture. But some has certainly been inherent in the effort to extract a large volume of savings from a very poor population.

The larger consequence is that the process of Marxian development risks, as non-Marxian development does not, the alienation of the people. One doubts that past governments of China are remembered with affection. But it is also the expert consensus that a majority of the Chinese people are scarcely pleased with their present rulers. They would not vote for them in an uninhibited poll. By contrast, India, after a decade of development, gave an overwhelming vote to the government that led the task. Had that government found it necessary to subtract the $7.3 billion it received in loans and grants from Western sources (as of 1963) from the meager incomes—an average of about $70 per year—of its own people, its popularity would certainly have suffered. One sees in India, in remarkably clear relief, the importance in the Western design of help in providing capital.

The second and equally substantial advantage of Western development is in the matter of agriculture. Industry, on the record at least, is fairly tolerant as to forms of economic and political organization. American industry works moderately well under private ownership. The most reluctant free-enterpriser must agree that the Soviets have made great industrial progress under socialism. So no decisive contrast can be registered in this sector of the economy. But the undeveloped country is, by definition, a pastoral or agrarian country. Its agricultural policy is, accordingly, vital. And it is still far from clear, as a practical matter, whether it is possible to socialize successfully a small-scale, densely populated, peasant agriculture.

In the Soviet Union, after nearly half a century, the agricultural problem has not been wholly solved. And in this area of economic activity at least, there is no serious talk by the Soviets of catching up with the United States. On the contrary, in agriculture each year we insouciantly extend our advantage in man-hour productivity without effort and rather to our regret. Outside the Soviet Union, agriculture has been even more of a problem. Poland and Yugoslavia have had to revert to private ownership. In China, by all external evidence, the effort to socialize agriculture brought a drastic crisis and considerable modification of the original design. Along with bad weather, it forced the Chinese to turn to the West for some of the largest food imports in history.

There are good reasons for this difficulty with agriculture. Farmers, when they are small and numerous, can, if they choose, defeat any system that is available for their control. The employees of a factory, like the men of an army, are subject to external discipline. Failure in performance can be detected, judged and penalized. The same rule holds for certain types of plantation agriculture. A scattered peasantry, carrying on the diverse tasks of crop and especially of livestock husbandry, cannot be so controlled and managed. Certainly it cannot be controlled if it disapproves of the system. And farmers have rarely, if ever, approved of any economic system which denied them ownership of land. The farmer has it within his powers, when working for others or for the state, to work at the mini-mum rather than the maximum, and the difference between the two is enormous. He can be made to work at his maximum by giving him land and rewarding

him with the fruits of his labor or some substantial share
to consume or exchange as he wishes. But this is to re--
store individual proprietorship—private capitalism—
which doctrine excludes.

One day the Marxian economies may succeed in so-
cializing agriculture. Certainly no effort is being
spared. And the ability of the small man in agriculture
to sabotage a system he dislikes or which treats him
badly is not confined to Communism. It is the reason
for the low productivity and backwardness of the lati-
fundia of Latin America and the feudal villages of
the Middle East. But the fact that independent agricultural proprietorship is accepted is the second clear advantage of Western development.

I come now to the principal disadvantage of Western
development. The Marxian alternative, I have noted,
emphasizes the destruction of the bonds that tie the
economy to the past. Our emphasis is on capital, education, technical assistance, and the other instruments
that promote change. Until recently, at least, we have
been tempted to suppose that any society is a platform on
which, given these missing elements, development can
be built.

In fact, institutions do chain economies to the past,
and the breaking of these chains is essential for
progress. The promise of drastic reform is a valid and
and an appealing part of the Marxian case. There
is no chance of agricultural development in the underdeveloped (and hence agricultural) country under
systems of absentee landlordism where the workers or

sharecroppers are confined by law and tradition to a minor share of a meager product. These feudal agricultural systems, moreover, extend their corrupting influence to government, to the provision of public or military sinecures to those who lack a claim on the land, to the milking of industrial enterprise, and to the destruction of the moral fiber of the society itself. "In our country," a guide in Lima once told me, "those who do the least work get the most money. I hear that in the United States it is the other way around. I believe it is a better system." Progress requires the radical elimination of retarding institutions. If elimination can be had from no other source, the Marxian alternative will sooner or later be tried. The revolution that is required here, we should remind ourselves, is less the Russian Revolution than the French Revolution.

There is one further and different point of comparison between the two systems, one which, unfortunately, has been much damaged by bad rhetoric. From the earliest days of their development, personal liberty, equal justice under law, and constitutional government have been important to Englishmen and to Americans. These things have not been the concern of everyone, but we have never supposed them to be a foible of an esoteric and privileged minority.

And so it is in the undeveloped country today. The Andean tenant and the landless worker in an Orissa village do have a preoccupying concern with keeping themselves fed. But a widespread yearning for the dignity of democratic and constitutional government is more common than is usually imagined. No people who live under a dictatorship ever feel themselves to be really first-class citizens.

And it is widely agreed that liberty and constitutional process are safer with the Western than with the Marxian alternative. We have not been nearly as consistent in our support of these as wisdom would have required. A curious inversion of intelligence has regularly caused those who regard themselves as the most learned and subtle in matters of foreign policy to urge the support of the most nauseous dictators. The consequences have been uniformly disastrous.[1]

On first assessment, then, the advantages of the non-Marxian alternative for the developing country are considerable. It promises at least a partial avoidance of the pain that for the poor country is inherent in finding savings for investment and growth. It promises an acceptable and viable system of agriculture rather than a certainly unpalatable and possibly unworkable one. And it offers personal liberty and constitutional process. Against this, the Marxian alternative promises a rigorous and effective attack on the institutions—the unproductive claims on revenue, and especially the feudal control of land—which exclude change.

But this is not a game where one can count the cards and decide the winner. Some cards count for more than others, and there is the unfortunate possibility, in our case, that some valuable cards will not get played.

[1] Except, I am led to add by way of amendment, to the architects of the policy. They are promoted and eventually retire with a high reputation for subtlety of view.

The Marxian promise can be decisive. That is because the things we offer are effective and attractive only after the retarding institutions are eliminated. In a country where land and other productive resources are held by and operated for the benefit of a slight minority, and where the apparatus of government serves principally to reinforce such privilege, aid is of no use. It will benefit not the many but the few. And the Western promise of independent proprietorship in agriculture is obviously nullified so long as land remains in the hands of the few. And personal liberty and constitutional government have little meaning in countries where government is of the privileged, by the corrupt, for the rich.

We have no alternative, in short, but to meet the Marxian promise to be rid of archaic and retarding institutions. I doubt that we can organize revolution. But we can place our influence solidly on the side of reform and movements toward reform. We can close our ears to the pleas of vested interest. If we do so, and reform follows, our cards give us a clear advantage. To be sure, we must play them all. We must make good on our promise of a less painful savings and investment process. We must give firm support to the small farmer. We must be clear in our commitment to constitutional process and personal liberty and we cannot suppose that these are wanted only by people of Anglo-Saxon origin of good income. We must not excuse dictatorship on grounds of anti-Communism or convenience or the absence of visible alternatives. This, to repeat, is one of the oldest and certainly the most myopic habit of our foreign policy, and its price we now know is disaster magnified by postponement.

These are highly practical matters. The first resort to the Marxian alternative in this hemisphere in Cuba was in a country where the concentration of wealth and land ownership was extreme, where these had extended a corrupting influence to economic life and to government, and where dictatorship had been endemic. This being the experience of Cubans with the Western model, it was not remarkable that so many were so little perturbed by the alternative. India, in face of formidable difficulties, is strongly committed to development on the Western model. That is because even in British India, and over the whole country at the time of independence, there was a strong attack on retarding institutions—on the feudal claims of princes, zamindars, and great landlords, and on a system of government which was in part an extension of this landed power. A substantial measure of peasant ownership replaced the old system, aid from outside eased the problem of supply capital, and people felt secure in the protection of constitutional guarantees and representative government.

Given the same advantages, we may reasonably assume that people elsewhere will opt for them.

IV. Development as a Process

THE DISCUSSION of economic development in the years since World War II can be compared in vigor with that which followed the publication of Smith's inquiry into *The Nature and Causes of the Wealth of Nations* in 1776 and to which in the following sixty or seventy years Bentham, Malthus, and John Stuart Mill, among others, made their notable contributions. The occasion is the same. At present, as then, nations are in the beginning stages of national development. The new countries of Asia and Africa are now concerned, as were those of Western Europe in the late eighteenth and early nineteenth centuries, with understanding the processes on which progress depends. Scholars in the more economically advanced countries have joined, and commonly led, the discussion. Americans can be proud of the particular intensity of the interest in the economics of development in these last years in the United States.

Both in the new states and in the old states there has been a considerable urgency about the recent discussion. Indeed, this has been a distinguishing feature. At least until the time of Marx, the problem of economic progress was explored with a measure of philosophical detachment. Now it has an imperative tone. The nineteenth century discussion was in a world that was rather proud of what was happening. The twentieth century discussion is in a world where much has happened but which feels that a great deal more must happen and very soon.

The recent discussion of development has also been remarkably more sophisticated. We now have growth models—hypotheses as to the nature of the process of economic growth, some of considerable mathematical refinement and a few that are wholly incomprehensible. Capital-output ratios and marginal capital-output ratios are now calculated on a mass production basis for the various components of five-, seven-, and ten-year plans and for perspective plans beyond. Specialized missions passing through the underdeveloped countries avoid each other only by adhering to closely planned schedules. There is a considerable sociology and a sizable anthropology of backwardness. We are told that Mill by the age of seven was master of the Greek classics. Were he now to reappear some ninety years after his death he might well decide, after seeing how elaborate are the matters on which he once wrote, to stay with Plato and Xenophon.

Yet it would be a mistake to identify complexity with completeness and sophistication with wisdom. There are some serious shortcomings in the modern discussion. And these become evident as we compare it with the earlier debate.

It is our pride that the recent discussion of development has been scientific—that terms and concepts have been rigorously defined and so employed that scholars working on different aspects of the problem can communicate with each other with some certainty, can correct each other as necessary, and by each adding his piece of knowledge to the common stock can thus add to the total wisdom. The earlier discussion was less precise but more grand. Smith, Malthus, Bentham, and Marx were builders of systems; they concerned themselves with the aggregate requirement of progress. The principles of good government, the inducements to individual performance, the role of popular enlightenment, the foundations of thrift, the effect of competition and of monopoly, the relation between social classes, the reasons why some people, notably the English, worked hard and others, notably the Irish, were idle, were all grist for their highly diversified mill. Anything that was deemed to have a bearing on economic advance came into the discussion. The only test was broad relevance to the questions: What made for economic progress? Or, on the other hand, what led to stagnation—to the much discussed stationary state?

The nineteenth century debate was conducted by a rather small number of men. By its nature it was confined to those who could make reasonable sense of large issues. Only great men could thus participate; we have often heard it said that each generation produces but one philosopher. The modern discussion, fortunately for all of us, has been much more democratic. That is because it has been concerned with the parts of the problem rather than the whole. Although men with a usefully cosmic view of society are scarce, many can contribute to knowledge of bits and pieces. It may not be easy to elucidate the relation of a philosophical or religious idea to economic change. But almost anyone can come up with some useful contention on the priority to be accorded to machine tools in the next Five-Year Plan.

Here, it seems to me, lies the weakness and even the danger of the current discussion of economic development. We have been enthusiastically and quite capably discussing the parts of the problem; we have paused all too infrequently to inquire whether the parts fit into a viable whole. We have looked at the things which contribute to economic development; we have given too little attention to inquiring whether they are being employed in a context that is favorable to development. As a result, we have probably wasted a good deal of time and effort doing things which were right in themselves but which made little or no contribution to progress because they were done in an environment which was inconsistent with advance.

Let me be more specific. In the years since World War II, and in the absence of any agreed diagnosis of the causes of poverty, as indicated in Chapter II, we have made two working assumptions. They are:

(1) That the world is divided between developed and underdeveloped countries. In the developed countries economic progress is easily within the powers of the country itself if it follows an intelligent economic

policy. Development is a good deal more difficult in the underdeveloped country. But it is also possible if an intelligent economic policy is pursued and certain missing components are supplied.

(2) The missing elements, on which there is a good deal of agreement, are modern technical knowledge or know-how, capital, specially trained manpower, and a sound plan for using capital, manpower, and technical knowledge. If these are provided, there will be progress.

The standard prescription for economic development proceeds directly from the foregoing. Technical assistance is obtained from abroad. Steps are taken to increase the supply of domestic savings and of capital from both domestic and foreign sources. Manpower is trained either at home or in the developed countries. A five-year or seven-year or ten-year plan is devised.

These steps will indeed be sound if the diagnosis of the development problem is sound. But it also follows that if the diagnosis is unsound, we will be having a good deal of waste motion in the world. It is my unhappy feeling that the diagnosis leaves a great deal to be desired. That it is more nearly valid for India or Pakistan than for other countries can be of only limited comfort even in these. If the job is bungled in one country, some damage is done in all. The Congress in particular has a not unnatural tendency to assume that error in one place is duplicated elsewhere. Let us look at the present assumptions in the context of some practical cases.

* * *

It is assumed that capital and technical knowledge are the missing elements. But in many of the newer African states national government is still in its beginning stages, and in parts of Latin America it has never been brought to a minimal level of efficiency. Under these circumstances, investment, whether public or private, is subject to the risks, uncertainties, tax vagaries, and the other aggressions of a poor public administration. It is idle to imagine that good development plans can be created or carried out without a reasonably good government to do it. And neither technical assistance nor trained technicians do well, or are even much needed, where administration is indifferent or bad. The best agricultural scientist cannot make much headway as adviser to a nonexistent agricultural ministry. The finest tax authority goes to waste if the minister does not believe in collecting taxes or has an overly developed feeling for his friends. The first task here is not to get capital or technicians but to build competent organs of public administration.

In the last century, nothing occupied a more prominent place among the requirements for economic and and social advance than public education and popular enlightenment. In the new states today, or the older ones without developed systems of popular education, schoolbooks must also come before machine tools. Popular education releases the energies not of the few but of the many. And it opens the way to technical knowledge. Literate people will see the need for getting machines. It is not so clear that machines will see the need for getting literate people. So under most circumstances popular education must also have priority over the dams, factories, and other furniture of capital development.

Finally, in many countries any serious look at the larger system must soon come to focus on the shortcomings of the social order, on arrangements under which wealth and political power are a monopoly of a small minority of the population and the masses, accordingly, are excluded from all incentives to improvement. As I have earlier noted, even the most eloquent agricultural extension expert cannot explain the advantage of growing two grains of wheat where but one flourished before, if the peasant knows that both will go inevitably to his landlord. The best-considered forms of agricultural investment or techniques of agricultural production are worthless, if the cultivator knows out of the experience of the ages that none of the gains will accrue to him.

In short, on even the most preliminary view of the problem, effective government, education, and social justice emerge as critically important. In many countries, in diagnosing the barriers to advance, it is lack of these that is of critical importance. And it follows that until these barriers are removed, little will come from capital investment and technical assistance. While plans may be big on paper, they will be small in result.

I have said that the present diagnosis of the causes of underdevelopment, with its stress on capital, technical assistance, and planning, does not fit a country such as India too badly. India has an effective government; there is a substantial measure of literacy; she has a backlog of administrative and entrepreneurial talent; there is a solid commitment to the goals of social justice and social progress. At the same time, the propensity to consume is high and the rate of saving is low, and the problem of capital supply is especially serious for that part which must be obtained from abroad. Under these circumstances, attention has naturally been focused on the question of financial support to investment.

We have here an important reason for our misapprehension of the problem of development. India is by far the largest and most populous of the underdeveloped countries, China apart. Her development has attracted more attention than that of any other country, partly because she has the most competent planners and the most articulate journalists and professors. India also has, despite their shortcomings, the best statistics, and, as all economists know, it is difficult to mount much of a discussion of development of a country where even imaginary gross national product data are unavailable. As a result, the world has come, in far greater degree than has been realized, to identify development as a whole with the experience of India, or, more accurately, India and Pakistan. Since capital and technically trained manpower are the limiting factors in these lands, they are assumed to be the limiting factors everywhere. Since competent planning is possible in India and Pakistan, it is assumed to be possible everywhere.

But the United States has also been responsible for some of the overemphasis on capital and technical know-how and talent. We have a healthy respect for money and its uses. While capital is not the limiting factor for the nation, it is for the individual enterprise or firm. And in the United States economic accomplishment depends not on the changing will of the government, not on winning the right social climate, not on finding literate workers, for these are available and assumed. Accomplishment depends on finding the capital and recruiting the engineers, scientists, and technicians. The world, in short, has generalized from the experience of the Asian subcontinent, and we have generalized from our own. Those who praise cooperation in these matters should observe that it extends even to misleading students of economic development.

What is the lesson? It is not that capital or technical assistance or technical training are unimportant, or that planning is a waste of time. India, where these are vitally important, is competent proof to the contrary. The lesson, to repeat, is that we cannot have one diagnosis of the causes of underdevelopment. Rather we must have the particular diagnosis which fits the particular country. And in few cases will the causes of backwardness or the requirements of progress be quite the same.

More specifically, we must recognize that economic development is a process,[1] one that extends in range from new nations of Africa, but slightly removed from their tribal structure, to the elaborate economic and

---

[1] Although his stages inevitably invite debate, as does his optimism about the so-called "take-off," Professor Rostow's most important contribution has been in moving consideration of the problem of development in this direction. (*The Stages of Economic Growth,* Cambridge, 1960.)

social apparatus of Western nations. At each stage along this continuum there is an appropriate policy for further advance. What is appropriate at one stage is wrong at another.

In the early stages it undoubtedly involves the building of organs of public administration and the provision of an educated minority, a nucleus of people who can build the system of public administration and, for that matter, everything else. Then comes the task of popular enlightenment. This enables the masses of the people to participate in economic activity. And it opens men's minds, as they can be opened in no other way, to new methods and new techniques. Apart from its cultural role, popular literacy is a highly efficient thing.[2] Needless to say, it is also the mainspring of popular aspiration. As such, it adds strongly to the desire for development. In these areas Peace Corps teaching can play a major role in the development task.

If development is to depend on popular participation, then there must be a system of popular rewards. There can be no effective advance if the masses of the people do not participate; man is not so constituted that he will bend his best energies for the enrichment of someone else. As literacy is economically efficient, so is social justice.

As one proceeds along the line, other requirements enter, and, depending on population and resource endowment, these will be different in different countries. Capital becomes the touchstone of development, the

[2] A matter to which I return in Chapter VII.

limiting factor, only in countries that are well along the line. Indeed, there is a distinct possibility that capital provided to countries in the earliest stages of development will be wasted. Only in a relatively sophisticated stage of development can it be well and wisely used in any considerable quantity.

At the last stop along this line are the so-called developed countries. In these—the United States, the United Kingdom, the USSR, Germany, France—capital ceases to be the limiting factor. Development becomes dependent on a complex of forces—scientific and technical skills and imagination, quality of working force, ability to make full use of available resources, clarity of national goals—which need not concern us here.

To see the process of development as a line along which the nations of the world are spaced, in their various stages of development, is to see both the process of and the policy for development with considerably enhanced clarity.

Thus it goes without saying that we can no longer speak of a common prescription for development. Any effort to offer such a general formula will be productive only of waste, frustration, and disappointment. And so, likewise, will be generalization from the experience of a country in one stage of development to the needs of a country in another stage. To generalize from the experience of the United States to the needs of India will be productive of error but so, equally, will generalization from the case of India to that of Brazil or Dahomey.

Instead, the need is for a design appropriate to the

particular stage in each country. In the early stages the
development plans will not be very elaborate; they will
be concerned with the first essentials of administrative
structure and with education and social reconstruction.
In these early stages, also, development encounters the
appalling problems of the closed circle. How does a
country without effective organs of public administration develop them, since bad government is not self-
correcting but self-perpetuating? How does a country
without an educated elite create one, since to extend
education takes educated people? How bring about social reform, when the class structure places political
power in the hands of those whose privileges most need
reform? These are intensely difficult questions, although perhaps not quite as difficult as they sound.
Other countries have broken out of the circle. And the
drive for development, in our day, is a force of considerable independent power, and it is not always kind to
those who, in defense of vested interest, stand in its
way. In any case, those who are concerned with development will not remove these obstacles by pretending
they do not exist.

As I have said, in countries that have conquered these
first problems, capital and technical knowledge become
the limiting factors. India's present need for capital is
not based on a low level of development. It is the result, as compared with the other new nations, of a relatively high level of cultural and political development
that enables her to use capital effectively. It is only at
this stage, where consideration must be given to how
scarce investment funds can be most effectively used and

where different uses of capital must be horizontally inte-
grated and phased over time, that planning becomes very
complex. It is wrong to imagine that the kind of planning that is done by India or Pakistan is essential for
nations in all stages of development. In earlier stages,
it is neither necessary nor possible.

V. Developing and Developed

DEVELOPING COUNTRIES, I suggest, can be thought of as beads being moved along a string. There is considerable advantage in being one of the countries that was first along that line. The nations that led the way—Britain, France, the United States, Germany—could take their achievements at their face value. Whatever they accomplished could be regarded with satisfaction. None did better. Exuberant pride in accomplishment was the mood of nineteenth century Britain. It is still in a considerable measure the mood of twentieth century America. The countries that came late, by contrast, have high and difficult standards not of their own making. They are faced always with comparisons—comparisons with the American or Soviet productive plant, comparisons with American or British living standards.

There is another troublesome matter for the late-comers. In a very poor arrangement of human affairs, development becomes easier the farther it proceeds. That is because each step in this process invariably makes the next one easier. Given no competent organs of public administration, it is hard to develop any. But a few good administrators will soon train others. Given no teachers, it is hard to launch an educational system. Given a few teachers, they too can train others, and given many teachers the training process becomes easy and almost automatic. Saving and capital accumulation are exceedingly painful in a poor country where the pressure of current need is very great. In a more affluent community, saving is much easier. In a rich country savings may, of course, be excessive.

The consequence of this arrangement is that the more developed countries are constantly widening their advantage over those that follow behind. On occasion, they blame those that follow for their poor performance. And to those that follow, progress must often seem disappointing. It would be well were we all to realize that if the pace of less favorably situated countries is slow, it is not necessarily because their efforts are less. Most likely it is because their task is so much greater.

To see the countries of the world not as divided between the developed and the underdeveloped but as spaced along a line representing various stages of development is essential if we are to have an accurate view of the problem of assistance. For when development is so regarded, we see that no group of countries is uniquely qualified to extend assistance and no other group is completely condemned to the role of recipient. Rather, each country has something to gain from those that are in front. And it has something to offer those that follow. The provision of aid is seen, as it should be seen, as a cooperative endeavor in which all countries may participate.

And while there will be differences in what is given

and what is received as we pass along the line, I am not sure that the contribution of the less developed countries is necessarily less. For the more developed countries, the provision of capital is an obvious form of assistance. But as countries such as India work out their problems of popular education, birth control, and land consolidation, this experience will be exceedingly valuable to those that follow along the line. I venture to think that India can often be a better teacher here than the United States. She has been much closer to the practical problem.

But let me rather stress the principle. To divide the world as between the aiding and the aided is both wrong and psychologically damaging. Development is a task in which many need help and as many have something to offer. This, henceforth, is how we must regard the task.

Now let me say a more specific word about borrowing and lending of resources and experience between countries in different positions along the development line. Given the different stages of development, nothing is more natural than that countries should look for guidance to the experience of those who have gone before. And nothing is more desirable than that those who have gone first should make both experience and tangible assistance available to those who come later. In the years since World War II, such borrowing and lending of experience and resources has become a commonplace. It is a matter on which the United States has taken a considerable lead. It will, I believe, be our best remembered contribution to the comity of nations. I have always wondered why so many ambitious men believe they can best win a reputation for wisdom by recommending ways of curtailing such assistance. Perhaps they confuse the audience and the claque.

Borrowing and lending between countries differently positioned along the development line is, however, a matter which calls for great judgment and great discrimination. The wrong things, as well as the right things, can be given or received. The experience of others can be wisely adapted and great good can come from it. And the practice of others can be unwisely adopted so as to do positive harm. Despite these difficulties and dangers, much of the borrowing and lending, especially of experience, that has gone on between developing countries since World War II has been exceedingly casual, as though no problem were involved. Again let me specify.

There are three things, which the more advanced country has, which can be borrowed by those following it along the line. They are (1) capital, (2) technology, (3) organization. The transmission of each of these between countries in different stages of development involves both rewards and dangers.

It is hard at first glance to imagine any of the less developed lands being damaged by an excess of capital. And, as I have noted, countries in the higher stages of development accumulate capital far more easily than those in the less advanced stages. This is one reason why lending between advanced and less advanced countries on concessional terms—at low or zero rates of interest and for long terms of repayment—should be considered

normal and natural. No one should be excessively im-
pressed by economic aid which is in the form of ten-year
loans at 7 percent. Few countries in any early stage of
development can easily pay the price of purely commercial credits.

But even loans at low or zero rates, or forthright grants
of capital, have their dangers. As noted, the ability to
use capital in any considerable volume is itself the result
of development. The provision of power and transportation to trained, literate, and socially emancipated people
is bound to be productive. The productivity is far less
certain if these things are provided to people who are
still enslaved by ignorance or a backward social system.

Even in a country such as India, which has reached the
stage where it can use capital in quantity, borrowing
from abroad can be a substitute for earning from abroad.
Export earnings depend on efficient and low-cost production. The poor country must take advantage of the
tendency for the more advanced nations to become
what Keynes once called "high-cost, high-living" countries. Any friend of India must view with some concern the rather uninspiring behavior of Indian exports in the last five years. At a roughly similar stage
in her industrialization, Japan had no alternative but
to force her products onto the markets of the world.
This was not a formula for universal popularity. But
it did provide the earnings for investment which in-
sured her further growth. It is doubtful if aid, however generous, can ever be a substitute for such earnings and for the independence and self-confidence that
they afford.

The borrowing of technology is also a subtle matter. In principle it is highly desirable. One advantage of being second in line is that the country so placed can take advantage of what has been worked out, often with considerable mental labor and cost, by those who have gone before. One must know, however, *why* the thing was worked out. Was it a step forward in a process or product of universal application? Or was it an adaptation to the requirements of advanced economic development itself? High-yielding maize hybrids, the Japanese method of rice cultivation, improved fertilizer use, the L-D process of steel production are advances of general application. They economize all resources. They are as appropriate and important for the less as for the more developed country. But much of the technology of the more advanced countries represents an accommodation to labor shortages or reflects the other special requirements of the more advanced economy. The mechanical cotton picker and the modern heavy farm tractor are innovations of this sort. Their use on the farms in the United States reflects the fact that labor for hire is exceedingly scarce. This technology should not be taken over by countries in the earlier stages of development. To do so is to waste scarce resources and handicap development and, much more than incidentally, to add to unemployment.

Thus, it is a mark of wise development planning to copy from the countries in the more advanced stages. And it is also a mark of wise planning not to do so. The distinction which I have just made between innovations of universal application and those which are merely adaptations to higher stages of development is not an easy one to apply. But it is more likely to be applied if the need for the distinction is at least recognized. Not long ago, in a neighboring Asian country where there is chronic unemployment and where wages are low, expensive automatic gates from abroad were being planned for railroad crossings. These are a necessary development in those countries where no one is any longer available for the reflective life of the railway gateman. But not here. Had the distinction I am making been more clearly in mind, considerable money would have been saved and the gatemen would have remained gratefully at their posts.

However, where imitation is appropriate, it should be unabashed and unashamed. This will not be applauded by the more advanced countries; they have often felt that such behavior by the newcomer is not quite sporting. The British in the last century spoke most disrespectfully of the imitative tendencies of the Germans; no sooner did Sheffield have something that was good than Solingen had the same thing in a cheaper model. More recently the Japanese and the Soviets have been similarly criticized. Those who come later should be undeterred by such complaints. They should take unblushing advantage of the paths that were broken by those who went first. The advantages of late arrival are all too few. Those that exist should be exploited.

So much for borrowing capital and technology. I come now to borrowing of organization, a term I use broadly to include government and its services, and educational, welfare, and economic organization. Here, in my view, the dangers are greatest of all. Such borrowing is now very casual. Because a particular organization or service—a government department, educational institution, subject of study, or agricultural or industrial service—exists in a more advanced country, it is imagined that it makes an important contribution to development. Therefore it should be re-created in the countries that are in the less advanced stages. It will aid their development too.

This line of reasoning, if such it may be called, is a rich source of error. Often, and I think usually, the organization and services of the more advanced country are not the cause of its development but the result. They reflect an accommodation to the needs of more advanced development or they are made possible by the level of development and income that country has reached. Injudicious and ill-considered borrowing and lending of such organization will not help development but will hinder it. The government of India is a complex and mysterious thing which reflects the great variety of tasks undertaken by India in her stage of development. An equally complex organization would be a major misfortune for one of the newer African states with, for the foreseeable future, a far simpler range of tasks. A great many features of the governmental, educational, agricultural, and industrial organization of the United States are not important for American development. They exist because a relatively advanced stage of development makes them necessary or, on occasion, because we can afford the unimportant. Their transfer

to the less developed lands is equally disastrous. If
luxuries of the educational curriculum, esoteric educational institutions, refined agricultural services, prefab-
ricated housing, and a wide range of public services are
adopted before their time, they will draw resources and
energies from the tasks that are strategically vital for
development. This is not beneficial; it is harmful. Let
me press the point.

A hundred years ago the development of the trans-
Mississippi plains in the United States called, above all
else, for a land policy which would get the land settled
and plowed and a transportation system which would
get the products to market. To this end the government surveyed the land, gave 160 acres to anyone who
had proved his good intentions by farming it for a few
months, and subsidized the building of railways. These
essentials being provided, development proceeded with
unexampled speed. It was our unquestioned good fortune that community education experts, grain marketing analysts, home economists, vocational counselors,
communications specialists, or public safety advisers had
not been invented. Had these existed, attention would
have been drawn from the strategically central tasks of
getting the farms settled and the railways built. And
they would have been a burden on the backs of people
who could not yet afford such luxuries.

Today in the United States these more elaborate
services can easily be afforded. And in the present stage
of our development, they may be needed. Transferred
to Africa, or to India, they may be as redundant and
even damaging as they would have been in the United

States in its comparable stage of economic development.

The burden of proof must be on those who propose the transfer of organization and services. It is a far more delicate business than we have imagined. This is a warning to those of us who have been lenders just as much as to those who have been borrowers, and perhaps more.

There is an assumption against which everyone responsible for an aid program must be on guard. It runs as follows: The United States is a developed country; it has land-grant colleges, extension specialists, institutes for educational research, and educational television. It follows that the country that seeks development must have these things. It does not follow at all. But neither is it easy to persuade the professional evangelist for one of these fields that it does not follow. In my personal experience, it is rather more probable that he (or she) will conclude that the person who counsels keeping things in phase is highly unimaginative.

I have dwelt on some misconceptions of the development problem—misconceptions which experience now allows us to correct. We should not be surprised that there have been errors. To mount a major attack on privation and backwardness is an enormously complex task. It was necessary that we simplify; and it was inevitable, perhaps, that oversimplification would lead to mistakes. It would have been a far greater error to postpone action and await a perfect view of the problem. And experience is a considerable teacher, even though, as Oscar Wilde once observed, it is also the name we give to our mistakes.

VI. Development Planning
and Practice

NOT LONG after World War II, on a mountaintop in Switzerland, a group of somewhat aging and wholly perturbed scholars gathered to survey the scene and consider what should be done about all of the talk of planning and postwar planning then so much in vogue. Many stories have been told of that gathering, most of them no doubt apocryphal. One is of a bitter debate over whether to take a stand, as a matter of principle, against the public ownership of naval vessels. On this, some of the most spirited opponents of planning were inclined to compromise. But the purists are held to have insisted that naval defense should be supplied by private enterprise through competitive bidding.

Whether this discussion took place or not, it should have, for it contains all of the outstanding characteristics of the debate over planning: the tendency to see it as a religious issue, as a test of faith rather than as a practical question of public policy; the tendency to see a conflict between the market and planning, although prices can be a very useful instrument of the planner; and the tendency, above all, to identify public ownership and planning. All of this has been a source of great confusion and, as a result of this and the curious tendency for all discussions of the subject to attract those who say the most and know the least, most people, on encountering the word "planning," decide to read no further. In general they are well advised.

Planning by national communities consists, first, in establishing selected objectives or goals and, second, in devising a method or design for reaching them. In the last century, the emerging industrial communities of Europe and North America accepted pretty much whatever fortune the miracle of economic progress brought them. We can agree that they did no planning, although it could be argued that, in the early years of the American republic, Alexander Hamilton's *Report on Manufactures* was the forerunner of the modern plan. In modern times, however, all advanced national communities have established fairly firm goals for themselves in matters of economic policy and have devised measures of greater or less efficiency for seeking to reach these goals. All can thus be said to plan. The United States holds before itself the need to keep unemployment below a certain maximum and to sustain a certain level of accomplishment, in relation to that of the Soviets, in defense and space exploration. It is also disposed to set itself a certain percentage rate of growth of Gross National Product, but there has never been agreement on what it should be, and only economists remember the current rate. As the United States sets as its goals, in many matters, keeping ahead of the Soviet Union, so the Soviet Union sets as its goals catching up

with the United States. In this aspect of planning, there
is an excellent reciprocal relationship between the two
countries. Each makes it impossible for the other to
succeed too easily.

The difference between modern national communities
is not in having a plan, but in the degree to which the
existence of the plan is avowed, in the formality with
which the goals are spelled out, and in the particular
techniques used to achieve the goals of the plan. The
United States, being officially an unplanned economy,
does not avow its planning. It also uses techniques appropriate to its particular stage of development. India,
Pakistan, Ceylon, are less reticent. And the techniques
are the rather different ones that serve a much less advanced stage of development.

I have elsewhere discussed the planning goal of the less
developed country; it is the improvement of the well-
being of the modal person. This goal is the counterpart
of the poverty of the poor and it is not only central but
total. Rich countries have the luxury of a choice of
goals; poor countries do not. My concern now is not
with the goals of planning but with the techniques for
achieving them. Here we encounter two closely inter-
related and much debated questions: first, the extent of
state initiative, as opposed to market incentive, that is
required for reaching planning goals; and second, the
extent to which state initiative requires public ownership of productive facilities.

On one area of state initiative, there is general agreement. Where something must be brought into exis-

tence which cannot readily be bought or sold and which is deemed so important that it ought to be available to everyone, then a direct action by the state is necessary. Such, for example, is the case of education or the provision of roads or the prevention of disease.

There is implicit but not explicit agreement on another field. When, to go a little distance for a phrase, a great leap forward is necessary, there is no alternative to a state initiative. For the development of atomic energy in the advanced countries, there was no alternative to government action. Similarly with space exploration. The initial passages to the moon will cost some tens of billions of dollars. This will almost certainly discourage the average tourist and prevent the business from soon being placed on a paying basis. Accordingly, apart from the hideous possibility of remaining at home, there is no alternative to government-sponsored moon travel. The old-fashioned subsonic jet passenger transport would not have existed except as a by-product of government-sponsored military development. The development of supersonic transport has had to wait on government initiative. One rewarding result of these necessities has been the discovery of how much government initiative is welcomed in a capitalist economy once it is discovered that capitalism cannot do the job.

Where, however, no great leap is involved, there is a choice between having the initiative with central authority or leaving it to the market. In the United States the government on at least one occasion intervened to increase steel output. Rather more frequently, it has ob-

tained more by leaving it to the market. Wheat production in the United States can be reduced—the problem
of increasing output has long been academic—either by
applying rigid controls or by allowing prices to fall in a
sufficiently painful degree.

There is also some choice between whether the operating units in areas of state initiative—the organiza-
tions which provide roads and schools, the firms which
organize the production of steel, atomic power, or supersonic aircraft—will be in public ownership or not.
The traditional theory of planning has normally held
that state leadership requires state ownership. Hence
the ancient association between planning and socialism
and, parenthetically, much of the suspicion aroused by
the word planning among private enterprisers. In practice, however, there can no longer be said to be any
rule. Public ownership of schools and roads is agreed.
Elsewhere there is some difficulty in telling what public
ownership really is. Thus, the United States, deferring
to conservative dislike of socialism, has numerous private corporations which, however, sell only to the state.
Their costs, prices, profits, and even executive salaries
and expense accounts are subject to a measure of
public restraint or review. The private ownership is
largely nominal, although all concerned will insist on it,
and some of the people involved are among our most
vehement anti-socialists. And in some areas—research
and development, atomic energy, electrical energy—
the United States does make extensive use of public
ownership.

By the same token, some countries make extensive

use of private ownership of productive units even in areas of state initiative. In Poland and Yugoslavia, the state plays a role of considerable importance in relation to agriculture. But the industry remains substantially in private ownership.

The unplanned economy makes use of market incentives—higher or lower prices and incomes—to induce changes in output. The same device is almost equally pervasive under planning. The difference is not in the instrument but rather in the goals it serves. Thus, efficiency in the Soviet Union is rewarded by paying profits to executives and workers. Workers are encouraged to greater effort or to less agreeable jobs or localities by the promise of better pay. This is a very practical matter. There is no reason for having an individual do something badly or unwillingly by public order when he will do it well and willingly in the pursuit of personal reward. Similar procedures are followed in the other planned economies. Yugoslavia has made especially imaginative use of market incentives. The use of such incentives, like the use of public ownership in the Western economies, is still resisted in some degree for reasons of faith, but in diminishing degree. In all of the advanced economies, there is an increasingly pragmatic selection of instruments—state initiative, various forms of state ownership, market incentives—for reaching goals.

The underdeveloped, even more than the developed country, needs to know where it is going. The problem of progress is one of elementary prevention of hunger, exposure, disease. So here the existence of a plan is an imperative. This is agreed even by countries which conceal their own commitment to planning. As a result, for the developing country the word planning has ceased to be controversial. Five-year plans are the invention, and were once the exclusive possession, of the Soviet Union. Now Americans and Western Europeans with impeccable credentials assemble in consortiums presided over with unquestioned respectability by the World Bank to consider financing for the five-year plans of India or Pakistan. The country which does not have goals, and a program for reaching these goals, is commonly assumed to be going nowhere. This may well be so.

There are three further reasons why in the beginning stages of economic development, planning takes on special importance. A number of the steps that have the highest priority at this stage—education and improved transport and communication—are, by their nature, among the things which require the initiative of the state. Nineteenth century governments, though they could contentedly accept whatever the market provided in other areas, took the lead in providing popular education and in building railways, roads, canals, and communications systems. No country has ever obtained a satisfactory school or road system by leaving it to the private sector. Most railroad systems have an extensive history of state initiative and subsidy. Matters are still the same for the new country now.

Secondly, the new country, like the developed country, must use state initiative where a long leap is required. But in the new countries the leaps are not the exception. I have noted that, where the development of supersonic travel or communication by way of earth satellites is involved, the developed countries turn without hesitation (and without criticism except occasionally for the delay) to state initiative. These are *their* big leaps where the market cannot be relied upon. But in India the development of a steel industry, or a heavy engineering industry, or even a watch industry involves a comparable leap. Accordingly, it requires a comparable initiative by the state. The setting up of the huge Fairless works of the U.S. Steel Corporation near Trenton was a comparatively commonplace response to market prospects. The establishment of a plant of similar proportions at Bokaro in India, although there is little doubt about the demand for the steel, is a mammoth undertaking, and without state action nothing would happen. Only individuals with a uniquely simple approach to the problems of economic development, or a peculiarly determined ambition for conservative applause, will make the mistake of generalizing from market performance in the developed country to what the market can accomplish in the poor country. It is no part of the good fortune of the poor country that this larger state initiative is required. As I stress elsewhere, economic development imposes, generally speaking, the greatest burdens on those governments that are least able to bear them. This is not a happy arrangement of human affairs but unfortunately there is no sign that such affairs were arranged for maximum convenience.

Finally, the poor country is under a particular compulsion to conserve resources. Not only is capital scarce but some of it comes free, or at concessional rates, as aid from abroad. Left to the market and the local distribution of income and demand, an undue amount would be invested in high-priced housing or the manufacture of expensive consumers' goods for the benefit of the well-to-do. And scarce resources in foreign exchange would slip away into luxury imports. All this is normal in the rich country but offensive in the poor. The United States in modern times has been the first to urge planning measures—licensing of luxury imports or taxation of luxury building—to prevent such waste. Conservative opponents of foreign aid are the first to complain when they hear about a recipient country importing Cadillacs.

Planning being peculiarly necessary in the poor country, I turn now to the requirements of a good plan. Of these, there seem to me to be four. And in present-day development planning, all are in some degree honored in the breach. The price of this neglect is considerable.

The first requirement is that the choice of instruments for the execution of the plan be pragmatic. In the developed countries, capitalist or communist, although the contest between the theologians and the practical men continues, the latter, as I have noted, are in the undoubted ascendency. In the United States, it is no longer necessary to find an appropriate doctrinal justification for a very extensive exercise of government initiative. One measure of the scope of this initiative is the proportion of the Gross National Product controlled and disposed of by the state. In the United States, this is approximately 20 percent of the total, as compared with 13 to 14 percent in India. There is similar pragmatism in the use of price and profit incentives across the Iron Curtain. Even British Socialists, in some ways the world's most ardent defenders of doctrine for the sake of doctrine, have largely given up on public ownership or have reduced their commitment to it to a purely symbolic level. That is because it no longer serves a clear purpose in the British economy. The common denominator of all this change is the tendency to accept, sometimes rather reluctantly, what works.

Nothing, I think, is more to be recommended to the less developed lands than the same salutary tendencies. And here, unlike the more industrialized countries East and West, the test of works, not faith, has still to make its way. China is far more purist in application of doctrine than the Soviet Union. Partly as a reflection of the high church rigor of British socialist doctrine, socialism *qua* socialism rather than what socialism accomplishes is still an objective of many of the former British territories. This means that the test of public or private ownership is not necessarily what best advances development. Rather, in some metaphysical sense, it is what advances a socialist pattern of society. As a result, economic performance is regularly sacrificed to doctrine. And the suggestion that a more pragmatic test would be wise is resisted with a good deal of moral indignation. One wing of the modern left prefers in practice to attack capitalism and accept poverty rather than have a greater measure of progress with a pragmatically mixed economy.

It is worth repeating once more, especially for the improvement of those who might take conservative comfort from this formulation, that a pragmatic course requires equally that public ownership be accepted where this is required. The test of what is practical works both ways.

The decision on other instruments should be equally pragmatic and here, also, there is room for improvement in the less developed lands. The purposeful use of price incentives and disincentives can be a major substitute for administrative effort and time. No one doubts that good prices to farmers—and it is wholly consistent with effective use of the price system that these be guaranteed by the state—are superior for increasing output to orders enforced by police and magistrates. But likewise high import prices, the result of high tariffs and realistic exchange rates, may be far more efficient than import licenses for rationing scarce foreign exchange. It may be wise to exclude luxuries by fiat. But ability and willingness to pay may not be a bad test of the effective use of capital goods imports. Similarly, high interest rates, testing again the need of the community for the investment, may be superior to a system of licenses and permissions as a device for rationing capital. High prices of imported capital or high interest rates may also usefully take the pressure off the planning system and thus play a useful supplementary role. The man who must pay the full price for imported goods has that much less incentive to offer bribes to obtain a license. Even where the price system works less precisely than a system of licenses, franchises, permissions, and orders, there may be a strong case for it because of its remarkable capacity for eliminating the costs of delay.

The second requirement of a good plan is that it be accommodated to the level of economic and cultural achievement of the country in question. In the beginning stages of development, plan creation is not properly a matter of economic planning at all; rather the goal is to build basic administrative organs, to develop the educational and basic cultural structure, and to get a viable and progressive social system. In Western Europe and the United States, following the French and American Revolutions, these steps laid the foundation for economic advance. The same steps following the Meiji restoration laid the same groundwork in Japan. In developing its Central Asian republics, the Soviets gave high priority to developing an effective system of provincial administration, to education, to providing a transportation system, and to getting the nomads into a settled system of agriculture.

It follows that, in the early stages of development, the task is not to set production targets and plan investment outlays. Rather it is to lay the administrative, social, and educational groundwork for such investment.

Only in later stages is detailed planning of investment in order. It belongs, relatively speaking, to a rather advanced state of development.

The third requirement of a good plan is a sense of strategy. This applies, particularly, to the fairly advanced countries just mentioned. The standard modern development plan is an investment plan. It reflects decisions on how best to employ scarce capital resources. Its primary goal is the thing that investment is assumed to accomplish, namely a specified and presumably adequate rate of economic growth. In this planning, a good deal of thought goes into the matching and phasing of the various segments of the plan—into insuring that kinds and amounts of steel being produced or imported will match requirements for steel in kind and amount, and that this balance between supply and requirements is maintained over time. Equally careful attention is accorded the supply of investment resources—the question of where, internally and externally, the capital is coming from. One can find little fault, in principle at least, with the way this part of the planning task is performed.

There is a grave danger, however, that such a plan will present all things as equally important. They are not. Some things are broadly catalytic in their role. Others are indispensable for improved well-being. Other things are merely passive and useful. A good plan must provide a strategy for economic advance. It is a well established fact that among angels virtue goes unnoticed. Equally if everything is held to be vital, the truly vital escapes attention.

By way of illustration, in an industrialized country a highly efficient transportation system and an economic and reliable source of power are indispensable. With these available, something is certain to happen; without them, one can be less sure . These industries provide the external economies of other industries. They make it possible for others to exist. In the somewhat different case of agriculture, while many things are useful, a few things are indispensable. Water, fertilizer, and improved seed can revolutionize agriculture. Other agricultural services, by contrast, have only a limited impact. Veterinary medicine, improved packaging, marketing advice, home economics may be useful but they will produce no major change.

Strong forces work against strategic concentration. In any country engaged in planning there is a relentless pressure on individuals, departments, and regions to have favorite enterprises included. To be outside the plan is to have a nasty sense of exclusion with practical financial consequences as well. The desire not to be accused of overlooking something is also strong. So there is a tendency for the plan to become not a plan but a list of all the things that should be done, that everyone would like to have done, or that anyone believes ought to be done or which might be a cause of criticism if overlooked. Specification of the things of strategic urgency is lost.

In the American colonies prior to independence and in the early years of the republic, there was no great surplus of food. The space between the mountains and the sea along the Atlantic was limited and not every-

where fertile; the demands for food and fodder sometimes exceeded its capacity and food had to be imported from Europe. A plan formulated along modern
lines for relieving this situation would have emphasized
the need for agricultural colleges, extension services,
veterinary services, plant breeding, better marketing,
control of insect pests, advanced horticulture, fish culture, and the provision of storage capacity for buffer
stocks. Doubtless also there would have been mention
of the need for improved transportation. But among
all the other excellent and useful ideas, this could easily
have been overlooked. In 1825, the State of New York
opened a canal which connected the black lands of the
West with the centers of population. On its completion,
the food shortage came to an end and there has been no
sign of recurrence. This canal was the strategic factor
in the plan. The importance of isolating and emphasiz-
ing the elements of strategic importance is not less in
the developing country today.

The fourth requirement of a good plan is that it emphasizes both the visible and the invisible dimensions
of industrial achievement. Like an iceberg, much of a
modern industrial society is out of sight. And, also like
an iceberg, the invisible part has the greatest capacity
for causing shipwreck. To get capital plant—railway
lines, coal mines, airplanes, oil rigs—into use is the visible achievement of development planning. To ensure
that this plant is efficiently used—that management is
independent and sound, and that in consequence product quality is good, cost of production low, and earnings

adequate for replacement and expansion of plant—is the much larger part of the task. This part lies below the surface. Nor is it sufficient that the developing country be only adequate in these respects. It must be more efficient than its older competitors. It was by low cost and efficient production that Germany and Japan won their places in the industrial constellation against the competition of the earlier arrivals. New industrial countries, such as Israel and Yugoslavia, have recently been making their bid in the same way. It is thus that both domestic and foreign earnings for further expansion are won.

I think it extremely important that the modern plan set firm targets, especially for publicly owned firms, for this invisible achievement. As valuable as firm targets for steel output are firm targets for man-hour productivity, costs, and returns. Goals so set become binding on all concerned. All are challenged to meet them. All have a sense of failure if there is a shortfall in performance. And there is, in addition, the highly practical fact that failure can be identified with those responsible. If there are no standards, then no one fails the examination. Promotion and honor accrue to all alike. Economic achievement was not meant to be that easy, and certainly not in a developing nation. Socialists are oddly reluctant to accept advice from non-socialists on what to believe. That is partly because they are so regularly advised to give up their belief in socialism. It may still be worth reminding all socialists, nonetheless, that the most damaging thing that has happened to the idea of public ownership is the growing belief, reinforced by numerous and visible practical examples, that it is shockingly inefficient.

In much of present planning, targets are set for visible physical accomplishment—for capacity in place or for production. This is the easiest and certainly the smallest part of the task. But targets are equally practical for managerial performance, labor productivity, costs and returns; all lend themselves admirably to objective measurement. It is of the greatest importance that the modern development plan be as complete in respect of these goals as any other.

VII. Education and Economic Development

In these last years, as the new countries of Asia and Africa have turned to the tasks of national development, they have had to decide what priority to accord to investment in education. Should it have the very highest priority? Is education a prerequisite to all other progress? Or should a certain economic base be provided first? Only as increased production income is available does good education become possible. Only from this will there be wherewithal to support schools and colleges and universities. Economic growth is necessary if a nation is to pay for schools and teachers.

This has been the question. It has been decided in various ways. Sometimes education has been given priority. Sometimes other forms of expenditure—roads, airports, dams—have been put first because they seemed the most pressing needs. Sometimes, to be sure, there has been no choice. Everything has been attempted in principle and nothing much accomplished in practice.

Still there is a problem of priority here and it is comparatively new. Uncertainty has entered with economics.

Economic development in our day has come to be regarded overwhelmingly as a problem in economic analysis. In economic analysis, the role of education is am-
biguous. This ambiguity has contributed in turn to
doubt and uncertainty as to what comes first.

We think of economic development as the investment of present resources for increased future production—the investment of savings for growth. We regularly measure the development effort of a country by
the volume of its investment—what it saves from its
own consumption, and what it borrows from consumers abroad, to invest in future increases in output. And
here is the problem, for education is both a form of consumption and a kind of investment. Like bread or
wine, it is something we use or consume. But, like a
dam or canal, it is something in which we invest to produce more in the future. This difference leads to very
different attitudes toward education in development.
When we think of education as a consumer service, it
becomes something on which we should save. Savings
are necessary for investment, and savings are obtained
by economizing on consumption, hence education is
something on which we should economize. But when
we think of education as an investment, it becomes
something not to be economized but emphasized. We
seek to expand investment. Hence we seek more educational investment. The resulting conflict in policy could
scarcely be sharper.

The contrasting attitudes which underlie this conflict
are evident in almost every discussion of education.

Convocation speakers the world around remind their highly indifferent audiences that man does not live by bread alone. The enrichment of the mind is as important as the nourishment of the body. Intellectual activity is properly pursued for its own sake; the poet, artist, or writer rightfully scorns economic gain as a test of performance. Because of their tendency to apply economic calculation to refreshment of the spirit and mind, Carlyle characterized economists as the learned professors of the dismal science. And who would say today that people should be rescued from the serfdom of ignorance only in order to make them more productive? In these attitudes, education, though a superior consumer good, is still a consumer good. Certainly it has nothing directly to do with production. And those who take a less uplifted view of matters righteously insist on the priority of ditches, dams, and fertilizer plants. For it is these that feed the poets.

But there is another view. Studies by Theodore Schultz, among others in the United States, have recently shown that outlays for education may bring large increases in production. By the kind of calculation that Carlyle most abhorred, they have shown that a dollar or a rupee invested in the intellectual improvement of human beings will often bring a greater increase in national income than a dollar or a rupee devoted to railways, dams, machine tools, or other tangible capital goods. To rescue farmers and workers from illiteracy may certainly be a goal in itself. But it is also a first indispensable step to any form of agricultural progress. Nowhere in the world, to paraphrase a point made previously, is there an illiterate peasantry that is progressive. Nowhere is there a literate peasantry that is not. Education, so viewed, is a highly productive form of investment.

And this is true of many kinds of education. Most men of perception, self-avowed or otherwise, agree on the importance of scientists and engineers for economic development. Machines, they will urge, are no more important than the men who make them, maintain them, or improve them. But the productivity of doctors and public health specialists is also very high. The suppression of malaria brings great increases in energy and output, as the experience of the last fifteen years has shown. (It also brings an astonishing output of babies, and, while we have talked of birth control in these last years, science has so far accomplished much more in promoting births than in preventing them.) The suppression of yaws and hookworm has a similar effect on productivity.

But not only scientists, engineers, and doctors are good educational investments. There are surprising returns to esoteric and even exotic forms of knowledge. The linguist obviously maintains the avenues to the technology of other cultures. Literacy leads on to a demand for writers who can supply its market. And the writer adds to Gross National Product in accordance with sales precisely as does the vegetable grower or printer. Not even the artist, as an object of investment, can be ignored. One of the most successful industries of modern India is motion picture production. This industry flourishes only in the presence of a secure artistic tradition in the theater, music, ballet, and the visual arts. It requires reasonably competent artists to produce bad pictures; it takes good ones to produce good pictures. No one ever invested in an artist with a view toward helping the balance of payments. Yet India's artistic tradition is a considerable source of foreign exchange.

In fact, education is of high importance as an object of immediate consumption and also as a form of investment for future production. It is neither consumption nor investment alone, *but both*. To look at education as a form of consumption, given the importance that the developing country attaches to investment, is to risk assigning it an unduly low priority. Some new countries have almost certainly done so. They have regarded their steel mills, dams, and fertilizer factories as the tangible manifestations of such development. Aswan, Volta, or Bhakra-Nangal *are* development. They get the discussion, the money, the visitors, the glow of pride. Well trained teachers may provide a greater promise of increased production, but they are not such tangible monuments to progress.

However, I have a feeling that this mistake is being corrected. Nor has the error been universal. India has held, on the whole, to the lesson of the nineteenth century, which is that education, or education abetted by honest and orderly government, comes first. The sound instinct of the Indian villager in wanting education for his children has usefully reinforced this wisdom. I doubt, however, that any country has yet accepted all of the implications of education as a form of development investment.

If education, and henceforth I intend to concentrate my attention specifically on advanced education, is regarded as a consumer service, we will naturally bring to it the attitudes that seemed appropriate to other forms of consumption. These include a high degree of permissiveness. The phrase "consumer sovereignty" is one of the oldest in economics; it implies the right of the consumer to choose between various forms of consumption. It implies, above all, the right to consume or not to consume as he wishes.

This notion of consumer sovereignty, when brought to education, suggests that the student who has reached the age of discretion, more or less, has the right to study or not to study as the consumer has the right to consume or not to consume. It implies that the choice lies with the individual and the individual alone. No one may interfere with or guide his sovereign choice in these matters. His is the ancient right to behave as a student. But if, in fact, the student is the privileged object of the investment of scarce resources, the matter is not so clear. Society has given him some of its savings. Surely he has a clear obligation to return to society the increased production that society expects and for which it has spent its scarce substance. The scarcer the resources, the greater, one imagines, is this obligation.

If education is viewed as a consumer good, it is the privilege of every individual to pursue the curriculum of his choice. Everyone has a right to an arts degree if that is the preferred and fashionable course of study. But if education is a form of investment, then the nature of the educational output becomes socially important. Attention must be accorded to the distribution of talent between engineering, science, medicine, agriculture, and other needed specialties. I am not going so far as to suggest that students should be forced into a profession which they do not prefer. And the planning of university specialization is an exceedingly difficult matter. But I am certainly suggesting that when education is viewed as an investment, serious thought must be given to the accommodation of students to need and the incentives and other arrangements by which this is brought about.

To view education as an investment will also have some bearing on college and university direction and administration. Colleges and universities must be responsive to the needs and requirements of economic and social advance and must be so organized as to make this possible. This means strong and responsive leadership by the faculty and its duly constituted representatives. The needs of the larger community must be effectively translated into curricula, courses, and good academic discipline. It is hard ever to take a stand against democracy. But the schoolmaster, at his best and in the most democratic countries, has always been a rather authoritarian figure. I do not believe that a university can be wholly successful unless it reposes strong and responsible power in those who teach, and unless those who teach delegate as needed to their own representatives. In recent times Latin American universities have been experimenting with highly democratic direction in which students, graduates, and faculty all participate more or less equally. It is a formula for deterioration into incoherence and chaos. The university is by nature an oligarchy of its faculty.

But I have no intention of allowing the faculty to escape without comment. It, too, has special responsibilities when education is viewed as a development outlay. By no means all of the traditional university practices and habits fit the requirements of the developing country. Thus, in most older university communities—mine is one—many faculty members have come to take a rather lofty view of teaching. We say that our primary task is research, or writing, or intellectual leadership. Students, we agree, are sufficiently privileged if they can see us passing in the street or listen thrice weekly to lectures that plagiarize ourselves and any other equally convenient source. These attitudes cannot be afforded if education is being tested by its productivity. Then the task of the teacher must be to shape and guide and instruct his students to ensure that they are indeed a more productive property. If he fails to do so, he is squandering scarce public resources.

Nor can subject matter or degrees be copied as a matter of course by the university in the developing countries from the older educational communities. Much of the economics that is taught in India is neither clinically concerned with Indian economic problems nor pragmatically with their solutions. Rather it is a fashionable elucidation of the sophisticated models and systems which are currently in fashion at Cambridge, the London School, or even at Harvard. As a layman I have sometimes wondered if medical education has been really adapted to the situation of the poor country. In the United States and Europe and, indeed, also in New Delhi, we yearn for doctors who are trained and totally trustworthy. The provision of such total training is the *sine qua non* of modern medical education. But in the developing country, with scarce resources, if we insist on these high standards for the few, may we not deny medical assistance to the many? Do we not get good doctors in the capitals at the price of having no one to set a broken leg or prescribe some simple painkiller in the villages?

The problem of investment is always to obtain the kind of capital most appropriate to requirement at the lowest cost. There is indication in fields as diverse as medicine and economics that a less costly form of capital, better adjusted to the requirements of the developing country, could in fact be obtained. Investment, to speak technically, could be rationalized. No one would urge the wrong tractors for the underdeveloped country merely because they exist in America or the Soviet Union. So with education.

But let me summarize and make a more general point. A developing country may rightly regard its outlays for education as an investment. The fact that these have also the characteristics of consumption, and are rewarding to the individual in their own right, must not be allowed to confuse the issue. That something is both a consumer service and a source of productive capital for the society does not detract at all from its importance as an investment. Rather it enhances that importance.

But when we consider education as an investment, we must consider it as purposefully as any other form of capital outlay. This the older and more developed countries do not necessarily do or need to do. Their traditions are different; wealth has made it possible for them to be much more easygoing. The new country cannot be so permissive toward those in whom it invests. They are a privileged group who must work to deserve their privileges. The teachers are custodians of scarce national resources which must not be wasted. The country must be sure that its educational investment is adapted to its needs.

In short, the developing country must consider its educational system in the light of the peculiar requirements of development. It cannot simply adapt from the older models. Having come late to development, it is the good fortune of the new countries that they can learn from others. But it is their misfortune that so much of what exists in other countries cannot be copied without serious cost. Adaptation, as I have earlier suggested, is as demanding in its own way as innovation.

VIII. Development
and the Industrial Corporation

THE WORLD's religions are, on the whole, unspecific on the nature of the economic system in the hereafter. Heaven, as it is vouchsafed to Christians, is known to employ gold as a paving material rather than as a medium of exchange, and its principal consumer products are stringed instruments. But we do not know the nature of the production mechanism, whether for making harps or other goods. (Some attention is given to fishing but this, characteristically, is a small-scale business.) However, if there is production of goods on any important scale, it is fairly certain that it will be carried on by an industrial firm or corporation. In this world, whether in India, the United States, the United Kingdom, or the Soviet Union, where any productive task must be performed, the firm is ubiquitous and inescapable. Accordingly it seems likely that it is also eternal.

The reason is simple: modern productive activity— the making of steel, aluminum, fertilizer, trucks, or machine tools—requires a complex blending of skills and talents in a complex mosaic of tasks and functions.

These skills and talents are not themselves rare, esoteric, or exceptional. If genius were required for economic activity, our situation would be serious, for genius is always scarce and the supply highly unpredictable. The peculiar achievement of the industrial firm is in dispensing with genius. It replaces it with an organization of the more predictably available talent of the community. It is a synthetic personality, in which many real personalities are combined, and its accomplishment is more than the sum of isolated individual contributions.

The corporate personality is not required for simple small-scale production such as most agriculture. This is within the capacity of the individual. It is not needed for most government functions—for the administration of justice, the collection of revenue, or the conduct of public education. These lend themselves to accomplishment within broad and stable rules. But the most characteristic feature of modern industry is the large scale of its capital plant, its considerable labor requirement, the complexity of its technology, and the changing claims which the modern market makes upon it. Here there cannot be predetermined rules for every contingency. There must, instead, be adaptation to ever-changing circumstances, and the success of the adaptation will depend on the blending of varieties of technical knowledge and experience possessed by numerous individuals. Here the corporation is essential. One must find a way by which individual talents and skills can function as a composite personality, and this the corporation accomplishes.

To see the corporation as a personality provides the prime clue to its administration. The individual or natural personality realizes itself only under conditions of liberty. To subject the behavior of the individual to the detailed surveillance of another is to obtain debased and inferior performance. Individual achievement is at its best when the individual has a clear set of goals and the means, including the knowledge, with which to pursue these goals under the stimulus of his own will. As with the individual personality, so with the corporate personality. The independence to pursue specified goals is vital; so is clear specification of the goals. Indeed, it is more important. Individuals are resilient and can resist and survive constraint. But autonomy is the only administrative arrangement that is consistent with the effective corporate being.

More specifically, the synthetic personality which we call the firm or corporation involves an intricate problem of cooperation and coordination among its parts. Much of this cooperation and coordination is accomplished automatically—it is the fruit of familiarity and confidence between the participants. One technician supplements his knowledge by resort to another; he knows to whom to turn and just how much confidence he can repose in the knowledge and judgment of the man whom he asks. The skilled worker similarly seeks help when his task takes him beyond the range of his own proficiency. This also he does on his own volition. The manager must know when and how to help, but no single manager ever manages in the sense that he makes all the decisions. In the successful corporation, decision-making is deeply inherent in the corporate being.

There are equally numerous and intricate problems of coordination along the time dimension in the industrial firm. Modern industrial processes are closely interdependent; delay in one place will ordinarily cause delay with cumulative effect elsewhere. There is, accordingly, a high premium on timely decision. Perhaps the most distinctive requirement of the industrial establishment, as compared with the ordinary government agency, is its dependence on prompt decision. In the industrial firm a bad decision made on time will not usually be as costly as a good decision made too late. The bad decision can often be reversed at low cost. The time lost waiting for the good decision can never be retrieved.

The need for autonomy and the peculiar vulnerability of the corporation to outside influence are directly related to these characteristics. If external intervention affects people, it will impair or upset the complex and subtle set of relationships on which effective cooperation and coordination depend. A couple of examples may be cited. The withdrawal of a known and proven man from the group in which he is participating and the substitution of another will mean at least temporary uncertainty as to the reliability of the newcomer's contribution and perhaps also of the decisions in which he is a participant. If personnel changes are subject to the formal rules of a civil service, there is considerable likelihood of recurrent and arbitrary interruptions of the cooperative process on which the successful corporate personality depends. The ordinary private corporation has full and autonomous control over personnel. This it will lose if it becomes subject to civil service procedures and therewith it loses one of its essential characteristics.

Again, it is evident that any external influence that delays decision can do great damage to coordination. If decisions on procurement, production methods, or prices must wait for an indeterminate period on higher authority, or are subject to unpredictable review and reversal by higher authority, then related and dependent action will also be delayed. The capacity to coordinate different actions will be lost. Again, the ability of the corporation to function as a synthetic personality is lost, for the power of decision associated with personality has been impaired.

I must emphasize that the corporate personality is damaged by both well-intentioned and ill-intentioned intervention. There may be little to choose between the two.

In both modern American and modern Soviet organization, there has been a large measure of accommodation to the requirements of the corporate personality for autonomy. The modern large American corporation enjoys almost complete independence from its stockholders, the principal source of external interference. While lip service is usually paid to democratic control by the owners, it is recognized, in practice, that any extensive and effective interference by stockholders in management would be exceedingly damaging. (As this is written, a law suit is pending against the principal owner of one of our large airlines to keep him from interfering with the management of the company he owns.) Some effort is made in the United States to accord a position of importance to the Board of Directors—the ultimate representative of the stockholders. So important are the men who sit on boards of directors of the large corporations that an effort must be made to believe that the boards are important. In many corporations they are strictly the creatures of management, appointed and (more rarely) discharged by the managers, and very docile creatures at that. At most, they ratify decisions of management, offer advice on major financial transactions, and stand by to intervene should the management become incompetent or corrupt. In all large and established corporations, custom severely excludes the board of directors from any effective association with operating and administrative decisions. Authority over production decision resides wholly within the corporation. This authority is also jealously defended against the state.

I do not speak with equal confidence of economies of the Soviet type. But certainly no theme has received more emphasis in recent times than the need for according managers the independence and autonomy that enables them to do their job. Soviet factory managers do not hesitate to stress to visitors the importance of such autonomy for the effective discharge of their responsibilities.

In the developing country, however, the autonomy

of the corporate personality encounters a stronger challenge. This is partly a matter of youth. Experience has not yet demonstrated the importance of protecting the corporate personality. On the contrary, the first instinct is to keep the organization on a rather tight rein to insure that it does not do something wrong. But the greater problem is that for reasons both of choice and necessity a good many corporations must operate in such countries under the direction of the state and in the democracies under the eye of parliamentary authority.

The public enterprise in the parliamentary democracy is publicly owned for a purpose. The most obvious purpose is to exercise a measure of democratic control over the enterprise. This control ensures that the firm's procedures and decisions will be in the public interest, that its decisions are sound and sensible and serve the general good. If there is no effort to exercise this control, some will surely say there is no purpose in public ownership. But plausible and innocent though this sounds, especially when we interject the magic phrase "democratic control" into the discussion, we have here a serious and often unsuspected contradiction. External interference with decision becomes an inherent aspect of the system with consequent effect on the corporate personality. And if individuals within the corporate organization are servants of a force outside the organization, they will no longer think automatically of the goals of the organization. They have, at best, a dual obligation; one part of the obligation runs to the firm

and the other to the external authority. One eye is on
the organization; the other is on the parliament or other
public authority. Decisions will not automatically be
attuned to the needs of the corporation. Some will be
related to the external political requirements. The
dual obligation is inconsistent with the requirements
of the corporate personality, which calls for the implicit
commitment of many people to the common goal.

The external authority has an even more damaging
effect on the time dimension of decision-making. I need
not mention again the importance of timeliness as compared with precision in industrial decisions. But the
man who must answer to a parliamentary committee or
brief a minister will always reserve to himself the right
to review the decisions that he must later defend. Moreover, executive departments and parliaments are
ordinarily aroused over the wrong decision. It is on
these that a man can score points and, hence, on which
others can lose points. The result is centralized decision
to avoid error but with the greater wastes of delay. This
is profoundly damaging to the corporate personality,
which must have decision-making authority where it
can be exercised with the optimal combination of ac-
curacy and expedition. Even if slow decisions are
criticized, they will not easily be expedited. For the
need to protect against the wrong as compared with the
untimely decision, even though the latter may be in-
trinsically the more damaging, will remain the prior
concern.

The problem, I repeat, is not of wisely motivated or
of ill-motivated intervention. Rather it is of anything

that interferes with or distorts and destroys the firm or corporate personality. This is a matter of the utmost importance, for external influence, with its impairment of autonomy, will always defend itself on the grounds of the wisdom or sincerity of its motivation. This is not a defense.

I have noted that the corporate body, like the individual, is effective only if it has liberty to pursue specified goals. This allows the full development of its personality. The second great problem of the public corporation in the parliamentary democracy concerns the goals. Paradoxically, while there is grave danger that parliamentary or other public authority will circumscribe the decision-making process and hence impair the personality of the firm, there is also danger that it will not be sufficiently powerful and firm in specifying goals. The standards of achievement of the publicly owned firm then will be insufficiently clear.

The goals of the modern industrial corporation in the United States or Western Europe are reasonably specific; broadly speaking, the most successful corporation is the one that makes a good profit and achieves a rate of growth greater than its rivals. (To be head of a profitable organization is an undoubted source of esteem in the United States, but higher honors are invariably accorded to the big firm which can also claim an impressive rate of expansion.) The setting of targets for production and profit, and the drive to meet and exceed these goals, is an established feature of Soviet planning.

The goals of the public corporation in the developing country have rarely been so clear. To maximize profits seems suspiciously like old-fashioned capitalism, which many of the new countries reject. The obligation to grow and expand has rarely been definite and firm. Subjective goals, such as the rendering of good service to the community or concern for workers, have been common. They have the handicap of their subjectivity—it is open to anyone to contend whether they are or are not being met. Those responsible often find it personally advantageous to spend more time asserting their good performance than demonstrating it.

There can be no doubt as to the solution. The industrial firm, by one designation or another, is inevitable for industrial development. It has a demanding personality; the major demand is an autonomy in everyday decision-making that is nearly absolute. That autonomy extends to the right to make mistakes, for error will often be the price, and a small one, for timeliness. The need for autonomy in the conduct of military operations is equally great. It is accorded as a matter of course. Nor can it be denied that generals have exercised to the full their privilege of making mistakes. In military theory, the delay that excludes error is the one unforgivable mistake. So with the corporation. In the United States, a few years ago, the Ford Motor Company produced an automobile which was a bad mistake. Great outlays were made on the theory that the public wanted a very large vehicle with something of the physiognomy of a surprised frog. The public was not

at all interested. Had this been a publicly owned corporation, the criticism would have been acute. Doubtless it would have led to the requirement that all changes
in car design should henceforth be submitted to a panel
of public reviewers, possibly a parliamentary committee.
The result might have been the avoidance of similar mistakes. But another certain result would have been recurrent, and in the end much more costly delays while
the panel resolved the unresolvable problems of automobile aesthetics.

Autonomy must include, subject only to the rules
which define abuse, the hiring and firing of personnel. It is flexibility here that makes possible the
complementing of one skill by another, one man's
knowledge by that of another, and which enables the
synthetic personality which we call the firm to do what
no individual can do. The intrusion of politics and
patronage into the public corporation is deeply sub-
versive of the subtle relationships on which an effective
development of this synthetic personality depends. But
so also will be the intrusion of civil service procedures
and routines. The latter may be admirably designed
to ensure equality of treatment for all employees. But
the effect can be to destroy the easy interpersonal ad-
justments and the automatic coordination on which effective operation depends. The world is full of unhappy choices, and in modern industrialism one of them
is between perfectly just rules and reasonably satisfactory performance. Autonomy in procurement, production, engineering, and all other decisions incident to
operations is equally an absolute.

But if the corporation must be protected in its personality from intrusion by outside authority upon its decisions, outside authority must be unremittingly firm in what it asks of the corporation. The goals it sets must be clear and utterly explicit. Success in all societies is in large measure its own reward, but there must never be any doubt as to what success consists of.

If I had to lay down a measure for performance for the publicly owned corporation in the developing country, it would be the earnings that it provides to put into its own expansion. Such expansion, in the given or related field and within the framework of plan, would be considered the prime goal of the public-sector firm. The most successful firm would be the one which by its efficiency and drive finds the earnings that allow it the greatest growth. Perhaps there are other goals that may be urged. But what is vital is that the goal, whatever it is, be specific, measurable, known to all, and firmly enforced.

Though the society should be wholly tolerant of errors that are within the framework of success, it should be wholly intolerant of failure to achieve the specified goals. Indeed, the nonachievement of goals, not the individual mistake, is the meaning of failure. Autonomy does not mean less public accountability. On the contrary, it means more. But it is accountability not for method, procedure, or individual action, but for result.

IX. A Postscript on Population

ONE THING many modern planners have done well. That is to get rid of inconveniently intractable problems by the process of pretending they do not exist or otherwise averting the eyes. This has worked with conspicuous success in the case of reactionary social and political institutions. Though it may be agreed in principle that feudal landlords, rapacious tax collectors, and corrupt dictators are capable of arresting all social and economic advance, it has often been possible to proceed in practice as though they did not exist.

Another prominent case of selective sight is population. In India, as this is written in 1963, there is great concern over the threat from China. That threat, perhaps, is not small. But I venture to think that the internal threat from increasing population, with its clear and very nearly present threat to the well-being of the average person, is greater. Indian population growth, abetted by a rapidly increasing life span (this has increased in the period 1951–1961 from 32 years to 45 years) is growing at the rate of at least 2.2 percent a year. There have been some recent indications that the rate of increase may be as high as 2.4 percent. These superficially unostentatious numerals mean an annual increment of 10 or 11 million people. This is more than the total population of Belgium. It is about equal to the population of Australia or Ceylon. The care and provisioning of this new population is the task which the Indian economy sets for itself each year. In the foreseeable future, there will be failure. The consequences will not be pleasant. There are not many other countries (China apart) where the population problem presents itself in quite such massive and relentless form. But there are other countries where it is also a wholly sufficient cause for alarm.

There are some countries—this is generally true of Europe and the United States—where more people mean more hands and more people at work and more products of all kinds to supply the added population. An increase in population adds to the labor force not to the pool of unemployed. And if it should add to unemployment, the latter can be corrected by an upward adjustment in the demand for goods. The newly available workers will be employed in existing agricultural or industrial plant. And the latter, if labor is available and the demand justifies it, will be expanded from the ample savings of the community and the rest of the labor will thus be absorbed.

This is the remedy open for the Keynesian unemployment of the West. It is the further misfortune of India, and similarly situated countries, that their unemployment is of a different kind. In general, the current agricultural base and the industrial and commercial superstructure cannot usefully accommodate any more people. The marginal productivity of agricultural workers, industrial workers, more shopkeepers, is not appreciably positive. In less stately language, there aren't enough places where people can do anything useful.

This means that new hands do not add to output. They either do not find jobs, or they displace someone who has work, or they split up one job into two. And an increase in demand is no remedy This does not increase the places where people can be employed. There is no more room in existing plant and in these countries the supply of new plant is limited by the limited supply of savings. Instead of the comparatively benign unemployment that yields to Keynesian remedies, we have in these countries the far more intractable Ricardian form that is limited by the available opportunities to work with any effect. If the increase in population exceeds the rate at which meager savings become available for investment, unemployment will increase relentlessly. This is the case, or very near to being the case, in modern India.

The only remedy is the control of population. This cannot wait on the initiative of the United States. In the United States birth control, to use the unadorned term, is a politically divisive issue. As a result, we will be slow in acting and even in urging. The countries immediately involved must take the lead.

The task must also, I venture, be put in the hands of

the right people. In every country there are two classes
of people, neither without merit; there are those who
see the ultimate problem and warn, and those who see
the immediate problem and act. Disarmament, in our
time, has been in the hands of the prophets and
philosophers; the proliferation of weapons has been in
the hands of the operators. The operators are engaged in increasing food supply or in arranging trans-
fers from the surplus to the hungry lands. Birth control is still in the hands of the philosophers and prophets.

A friend of mine who is undoubtedly an operator pro-
poses that the government of India acquire a hundred
helicopters. From these it would bombard every village
every hundred days with a supply of elementary male
contraceptives, a graphic picture on their use, and a
warning that in families beyond two, any further preg-
nancies would be taken as *prima facie* evidence of
failure to employ the new equipment. This would make
the male parent subject to heavy fine, a radical increase
in taxes, public obloquy, or all three combined. I doubt
that this is the right procedure as, in fact, does he; the
technique seems a little dramatic and the sanctions
rather Draconian for a parliamentary democracy. But it
is the way the mind of the operator functions; we would
not, of course, be at all surprised were such measures
and sanctions recommended in a bad locust year. The
danger to the food supply from locusts is, by comparison,
quite minor.

The important thing is that the population problem
must now go to those who act. There can be no further
rewards, either in this world or the next, to those who

believe they have accomplished something by braving controversy and proclaiming their support of birth control. (There can be no reward for those to whom the subject is an opportunity to travel and attend conferences.) Nor ought action be delayed by wishful talk of an inexpensive pill or like miracle. The nations menaced by the population explosion must now settle on the most practical contraceptive method now available, produce and make that contraceptive available in adequate mass, get it into use and judge the success of the effort by results—by what happens to the birthrate.

Index

Index

SENTRY EDITIONS

(continued on next page)
SE 3